FUNDAMENTALS OF ACCOUNTING INFORMATION SYSTEMS

AN INTERNAL CONTROL APPROACH

GRACE F. JOHNSON

NA

NorthAmerican
Business Press

Atlanta – Seattle – South Florida – Toronto

Atlanta, Georgia
Seattle, Washington
South Florida
Toronto, Canada

Fundamentals of Accounting Information Systems: An Internal Control Approach
ISBN: 9780988919396
© 2013 All Rights Reserved.

Along with trade books for various business disciplines, the North American Business Press also publishes a variety of academic-peer reviewed journals.

Library of Congress Control Number:2013946530

Library of Congress
Cataloging in Publication Division
101 Independence Ave., SE
Washington, DC 20540-4320

Printed in theUnited States of America

Introduction

Fundamentals of Accounting Information Systems: An Internal Control Approach introduces students to the foundations of accounting information systems: how data flows through various accounting subsystems and the manner in which it is processed and converted into output for users. Written in an informal and conversational style, this textbook emphasizes the role of internal controls in accounting information systems alongside discussions of business process data flows. Examples and illustrations deal with entities of various sizes and in different industries, including not-for-profit and government organizations. The connection between basic business processes and accounting information systems is explored in computerized and semi-computerized environments.

The textbook begins with overviews of internal control concepts, flowcharting, and business processes. Later chapters focus on specific business processes and the way data moves in and between them. These business process chapters include a capstone assignment, created so students will draw on the core questions in each chapter and apply them in a new situation.

Acknowledgments

The first draft of this textbook was written during my 2009-2010 sabbatical. I am grateful for having the time to think about and work on this project and thank the members of the 2008-2009 Marietta College Faculty Development Committee and Provost Rita Smith Kipp for approving my sabbatical proposal. My friend and colleague Ed Osborne taught my accounting courses during my absence that year. While on sabbatical in Korea, Dean Jung Sung-chang, Associate Dean Koh Jun, and MBA Program Director Park Mi-jeong at Chonnam National University's Graduate School of Business provided me with everything a visiting professor could ask for. I deeply appreciate your hospitality, the privilege to be part of your team, and the comfortable environment in which to dedicate myself to my work. And special thanks to The Magnificent Seven (Bev, Craig, Jim, Marilee, Mark, Nicole, and Tager), Soon Suk, and Gyu-seog for your friendship and support during the days – good and bad – of my sabbatical.

I take full responsibility for all errors and omissions.

Grace F. Johnson
Marietta, Ohio
November 3, 2013

About the Author

Earning her BS in Business Administration and Master of Accountancy from the University of South Florida, Professor Grace F. Johnson, CPA, is McCoy Professor of Management and Accounting at Marietta College, Marietta, Ohio, and is affiliated with the College's Asian Studies Program. Professor Johnson teaches courses in financial accounting, intermediate accounting, accounting information systems, and accounting research. Her work has appeared in The CPA Journal, Journal of Higher Education Theory and Practice, Decision Management, Journal of Education for Business, Journal of Modern Accounting and Auditing, Journal of Instructional Pedagogies, and Journal of E-Business.

She has taught and done research in Brazil, China, and South Korea. Professor Johnson is a member of the board of directors of the North American Accounting Society and a member of the West Virginia Society of CPAs.

Previous textbooks by Grace Johnson include Information Technology in Accounting Using Pacioli (South-Western) and, co-authored with André Sathler Guimarães, Sistemas de Informações: Administração em Tempo Real (Qualitymark-Brazil).

Table of Contents

Chapter 1

An overview of accounting information systems

Chapter Core Questions

1. How is an entity's accounting information system related to its business processes?
2. What are the objectives of a system of internal control?
3. Why must accounting information possess certain descriptive qualities?

Introduction

I am writing this chapter on a Hanok Airlines flight from San Francisco to Seoul. Settled here in seat 19G, drinking tea and glancing out the window at a clear blue sky, I am also reflecting on the series of interconnected business transactions for Hanok Airlines that led to my presence on this flight today. What are some of these transactions and how does the topic of **accounting information systems** (AIS) relate to them?

Accounting information systems: a collection of people, technology, and activities that collect, process, store, and communicate accounting information to internal and external users.

STOP. Think about this question. Now find a classmate or two with whom you can brainstorm ideas. Jot down your ideas in a two-column table that looks something like this:

Hanok's business transaction	Accounting information system impact

Now let's examine what your classmates and you discussed. Recall from your introductory financial accounting and intermediate financial accounting courses that a **transaction** differs from an **event**. A transaction has an immediate and direct financial statement effect on an entity (and these take place in for-profit, not-for-profit, and government organizations). An event is an occurrence that does not impact the financial statements and for which no journal entry is needed.

To start with, Hanok Airlines sold an economy-class seat when I booked my flight online. But was it really a sale for Hanok? I made my reservation about five weeks in advance of the flight. Once again, consider your financial accounting fundamentals. The journal entry at the time of the booking would have looked something like this:

8/23/2011	Cash	$1,600	
	Deferred Ticket Revenue		$1,600
	To record reservation for Columbus-Seoul ticket		

Although not a GAAP revenue-earning transaction at the time of the booking, my reservation would have been recognized as a liability (unearned revenue) by Hanok Airlines and the data updated in its information system. As the date of my flight approached, Hanok Airlines would communicate with its catering vendor that the passenger in 19G requested an Asian vegetarian meal for the San Francisco-Seoul flight segment. Upon delivery of that meal on the date of the flight, Hanok would incur in-flight food expenses and record an account payable to the catering vendor; these transactions would increase Hanok's operating expenses and payables.

What other expenses would the airline incur on the flight date? From the gate workers to ground crew, flight attendants, pilots, and other Hanok Airlines staffers, all are laboring that day to permit my flight to leave on time and safely fly to its destination. Hanok incurs a variety of payroll expenses, payroll-related taxes, and payroll payables. And don't forget the meals and beverages being consumed by the passengers on my flight. That's another transaction to recognize as Hanok records more in-flight food expense and a payable to its supplier. In addition, Hanok Airlines – like all other airlines – incurs fees payable to numerous airport authorities for the right to lease space and gates at airports. As well, these transactions generate expenses and payables for Hanok. Finally, let's return to that matter of the revenue. Hanok earns revenue for the outbound Columbus – Seoul flight. This transaction reduces the liability account Deferred Ticket Revenue and increases the revenue account Passenger Revenue.

In review, my reservation and the related transactions on the day of the flight affected Hanok's accounting information system in the following ways:

Hanok's business transaction	Accounting information system impact
Hanok processes reservation for roundtrip flight	Reservations: cash and a deferred liability
Hanok orders vegetarian meal from catering vendor	Vendor: purchasing
Hanok receives vegetarian meal on flight date	Vendor: in-flight food expense and accounts payable
Hanok staffers perform their jobs on day of flight	Payroll: various payroll and tax expenses and payroll and taxes payable
Hanok receives other passengers' meals and beverages on flight date	Vendor: in-flight food expense and accounts payable
Hanok incurs airport occupancy and gate fees	Operations: expenses and accounts payable
Hanok earns revenue flying passengers to Seoul	Revenue: deferred liability and earned passenger revenue

Every day entities conduct business transactions, the financial impact of which triggers entries to accounts in the general ledger, subsidiary ledgers, and various accounting information subsystems. The goal of this textbook is to help you understand how accounting information systems collect and communicate accounting data to users. These users are generally internal users (*e.g.* staffers, management) but also include external users (*e.g.* customers, suppliers, auditors, stockholders, regulators, media). Our textbook also incorporates a significant amount of material on a topic called **internal control**. As you will learn in Chapter 2 and subsequent chapters, strong internal controls underlie the effectiveness of an entity's accounting information system.

Chapter Core Question 1: How is an entity's accounting information system related to its business processes?

The Accounting Information System and Its Relationship to Business Processes

The phrase *accounting information system* (AIS) frequently serves as a generic phrase for the software and hardware used by an entity to capture accounting data, process and store it, and communicate the output to system users. An AIS typically includes a collection of applications and databases serving the work of staffers in various **business processes** in the entity such as accounting and finance, marketing, human resources, operations, sales, purchasing, and production. However, the system does not have to be fully computerized. Transaction data in the smallest of entities might be maintained using paper and pencil and the related financial statements created manually or using spreadsheets. Regardless of the form it takes, this data supports internal users' daily, mid-range, and long-run decision making. As well, the data is used to generate general purpose financial statements for external users (primarily investors and creditors).

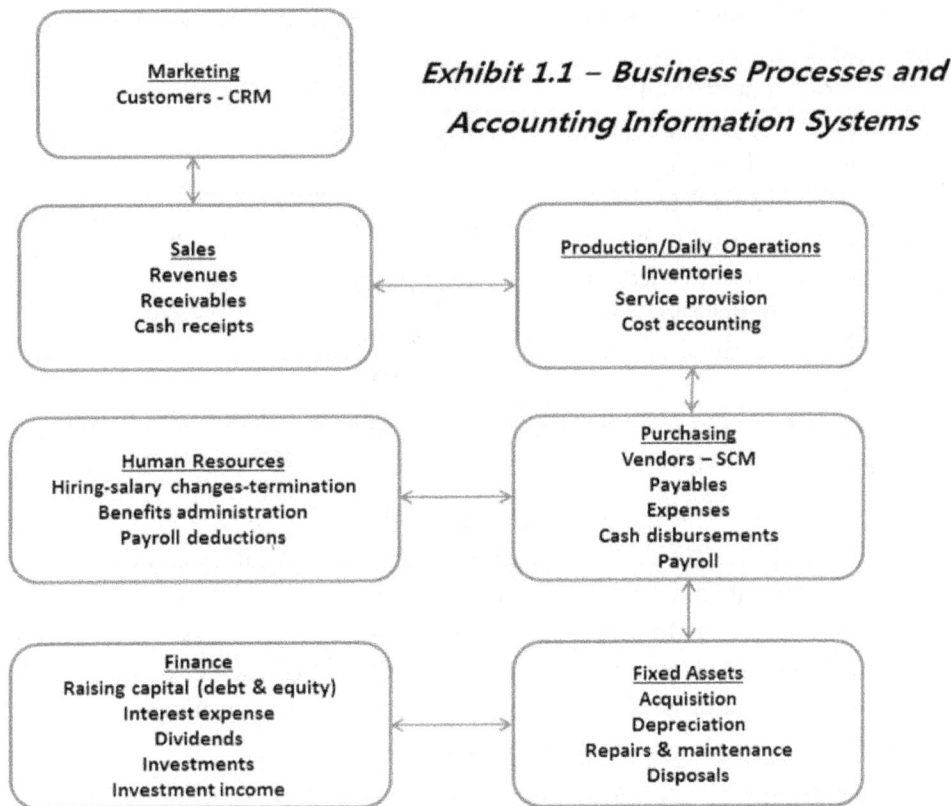

Exhibit 1.1 – Business Processes and Accounting Information Systems

Exhibit 1.1 shows the relationships among various business processes and accounting information systems. In larger entities, users frequently access data from various business process modules contained in an enterprise information system (*e.g.* SAP, Oracle, or NetSuite). In smaller entities, the information system could be as rudimentary as several spreadsheets used alongside basic functions of small business accounting software such as

QuickBooks or Peachtree. In the smallest entities, the AIS might not be computerized at all and merely rely on handwritten records and source documents.

Regardless of size, structure of accounting information system, or business process complexity, all entities must develop effective tasks to gather, process, store, and communicate the accounting data. Users depend on accurate and timely data from the AIS as inputs to their daily, mid-term, and long range decisions. A reliable AIS and strong internal controls enhance users' confidence in the data.

Chapter Core Question 2: What are the objectives of a system of internal control?

A Few Words About Internal Control

In the next chapter we will deal with the topic of internal control more fully. But right now, think about the meaning of internal control: *it is a collection of people, policies, and practices that (a) safeguard entity resources (b) encourage production of accurate accounting records and related financial statements, (c) promote achievement of management's goals and objectives, and (d) ensure conformance with external regulators' rules.* Exhibit 1.2 shows these four objectives of a system of internal control.

On the surface, implementing internal controls in an entity might seem to require a lot of extra effort, time, and money. But an overarching principle related to internal control design is to not allow the cost of the control to exceed the benefit of having it in place (cost-benefit rule). For example, why would you spend $37,000 per year to hire someone (plus the related employment taxes and benefits that must be incurred) to guard a room in which some of your company's raw materials are temporarily stored until needed for production? If the estimated financial loss (it's called **exposure** in the internal control vocabulary) is estimated at just $1,500 of materials per year, you'd never want to spend close to $50,000 to protect against a $1,500 loss, would you?

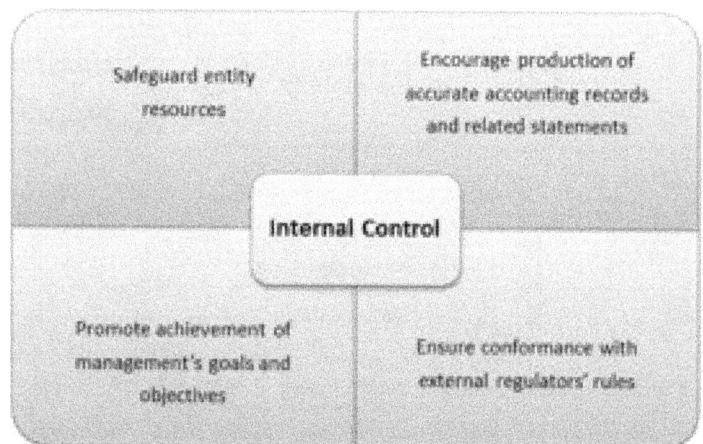
Exhibit 1.2 – Understanding the purposes of internal control

So why put into practice a system of internal controls? Without them, an entity is vulnerable to customer theft and fraud as well as misuse of resources and theft from its staff. Without internal controls, how would a publicly-held company know whether it is filing its SEC Form 10-Q on time? Would an entity know if it is properly disposing of its retired assets according to corporate policies? Can an investor have confidence in the information reported in the annual financial statements she's reading? Would the trustees of a non-profit organization be confident that the executive director isn't redirecting organization funds for his personal use? Internal controls help entities in practical ways such as these and more.

Chapter Core Question 3: Why must accounting information possess certain descriptive qualities?

The Descriptive Qualities of Accounting Information

When Hanok Airlines' financial analysts, for example, want to evaluate a particular route for its profitability, they must have confidence that the data gathered, processed, and communicated by the AIS is up-to-date, accurate, and complete. Only when the information can be relied upon and is relevant will the resulting business decisions be trusted. Refer to the Financial Accounting Standards Board's Conceptual Framework, Statement of Financial Accounting Concepts No. 8. In Chapter 3, *Qualitative Characteristics of Useful Financial Information*, the FASB identifies and explains the necessary features that must be possessed by accounting information. You studied these characteristics in Intermediate Accounting and they are worth reviewing from an AIS perspective. The fundamental – or essential – qualitative characteristics are relevance and faithful representation of the transaction[1]. Enhancing qualitative characteristics include comparability, verifiability, timeliness, and understandability[2].

The information's usefulness to the Hanok financial analysts depends on its being related and relevant to the decision they need to make. When the analysts query their AIS to retrieve the route's RASM (revenue per available seat mile), the analysts expect the data to reflect only passenger revenues and not revenues from other sources such as cargo revenue or interest revenue. If revenues from other sources were combined and reported by the AIS, the information would be neither relevant nor faithfully represent the asked-for transaction data, passenger seat revenue. Further, the RASM data should be determined using the same practices and methods in the current period as it was in previous periods (comparability). If others had the data available to them, the RASM calculation should be the same as determined by Hanok's AIS (verifiability). In addition, the analysts should be able to access the most currently available accounting data at the moment they need it (timeliness). And to promote good decision making using this information, it needs to be presented in a manner that's easy to comprehend (understandability).

How can AIS users be confident that the data contained therein exhibits these features? Controls must be in place and followed to promote accurate data creation and modification only by authorized users. Data must be reviewed and refreshed as needed for particular applications only by those approved to undertake such tasks. Recall that our introduction to internal controls identifies *encourages production of accurate accounting records and related financial statements* as one of the four objectives of a system of internal control.

In Summary

Whether you'll use accounting information systems in your work as an accountant or financial analyst, in the role of an internal or external auditor, or as a designer of an accounting information system, a fundamental understanding of how accounting data moves through the system – and the internal control over it – is critical. As a user, it will help you understand how the data you work with was entered and processed. As an auditor, you'll want to determine the level of internal control over the data and processing so you can properly design procedures for your audit. In the designer role, you must see how data moves and the actions performed on the data to suggest and implement efficacious changes to the system.

The accounting information system is closely linked with many business processes, including the key processes related to revenues, expenses, production, and operations. Business transactions recorded in the AIS are used by staffers throughout the entity for their short, medium, and long-term decisions.

A strong system of internal control lends assurances to users of the accounting information system that the data contained therein can be relied upon and is up-to-date. These characteristics are very desirable in the data used to make business decisions.

---

1   *Statement of Financial Accounting Concepts No. 8*, Conceptual Framework for Financial Reporting, Chapters 1 and 3. Financial Accounting Standards Board, Norwalk, CT, Sept. 2010, p. 16. Available at: http://www.fasb.org/jsp/FASB/Page/SectionPage&cid=1176156317989

2   *Statement of Financial Accounting Concepts No. 8*, Conceptual Framework for Financial Reporting, Chapters 1 and 3. Financial Accounting Standards Board, Norwalk, CT, Sept. 2010, p. 19. Available at: http://www.fasb.org/jsp/FASB/Page/SectionPage&cid=1176156317989

Now that you've had a taste of three central AIS topics –business processes, internal controls, and the descriptive qualities of accounting information – the chapters that follow dedicate more time in aiding you to understand and use them. The next chapter covers a critical area in accounting information systems: internal control.

Chapter Core Vocabulary

Accounting information systems – a collection of people, technology, and activities that collect, process, store, and communicate accounting information (primarily financial in nature) to internal and external users.

Business processes – collections of related tasks or activities undertaken to carry out particular functions in business. These include, but are not limited to, marketing, human resources, sales, production and operations, purchasing, finance, and fixed assets.

Event – an occurrence or happening that does not require a journal entry to update an entity's financial records. An event will not cause changes to an entity's general ledger or financial statements, whereas a transaction increases and decreases balances in the ledger and on the financial statements.

Exposure – a financial total equaling the probability of a loss of entity resources times their estimated dollar amount of the loss.

Internal control – a collection of people, policies, and practices that (a) safeguard entity resources, (b) encourage production of accurate accounting records and related financial statements, (c) promote achievement of management's goals and objectives, and (d) ensure conformance with external regulators' rules.

Transaction – an exchange between an entity and one or more players that is the source of a journal entry recorded in the entity's general ledger or subsidiary ledgers. A transaction has a financial statement impact, whereas an event *does not*.

Chapter 2

Internal control: the essentials

Chapter Core Questions

1. What are the objectives of a system of internal control?
2. What are some of the noteworthy pronouncements contributing to current ideas about internal control?
3. What is the ASSRAV internal control toolkit and how is it used?

Introduction

It's a cold and snowy morning in January 2009. You grab a cup of hot chocolate and sit down at your desk, open a web browser, and log on to your *Wall Street Journal* subscription. Across the top of the screen is a large headline about the Satyam Computer Services accounting scandal. It captures your attention as it does the attention of businesspeople in India and across the world. It's hard to imagine how Satyam's then-chairman, B. Ramalinga Raju, had fraudulently overstated the company's reported revenues for the previous few years and inflated – in excess of $1-billion – the amount of cash shown by the company on its balance sheet[3].

In the case of Satyam, the problems with **internal control** had their source at the very top of the corporate hierarchy. These vulnerabilities and weaknesses are difficult to handle, mainly because the actions of the people involved aren't easily caught or restricted by authorizations, a segregation of duties, or supervision. After all, who is there to approve instructions given by the chairman and chief executive officer?

Although challenging to exercise control over a company's executives, the Satyam fraud highlights an essential facet of an entity's internal controls: something called the *control environment*. As we'll review in a later section of this chapter, the attitudes of staffers and management about fraud and internal control play a major part in the efficacy of an entity's efforts to create a culture where internal control is taken seriously. And if businesspeople don't concur with the idea that good internal controls are good for business, the existence of government regulations and **best practices** might apply pressure on entities to adopt solid systems of internal control.

The sections that follow explain the purpose of internal controls, review key authoritative sources on internal control, and introduce an internal control toolkit you can use to evaluate, design, and implement internal controls in an entity.

---

3   Guha, R. and D. Gupta. 2009. "Satyam Chief Looks to Rebuild Brand as Uncertainty Dissipates". The Wall Street Journal. July 15.

Chapter Core Question 1: What are the objectives of a system of internal control?

A System of Internal Control and Its Objectives

As Satyam Computer Services Ltd. discovered, a lapse in internal control can cost the company in terms of lost reputation, customers, jobs, and ultimately, the loss of the company itself (it was acquired by Mahindra in September 2009)[4]. Recall from Chapter 1 that a system of internal control is comprised of people, policies, and practices. The goal for any system of internal control is to support the entity's business processes. It does this in four ways: (a) safeguarding entity resources, (b) encouraging production of accurate accounting records and related statements, (c) promoting achievement of management's goals and objectives, and (d) ensuring conformance with external regulators' rules. You were introduced to these objectives in Chapter 1. Exhibit 2.1 is the same as Exhibit 2.1 (page 18), graphically depicting these four objectives of a system of internal control.

Exhibit 2.1 – Objectives of a system of internal control

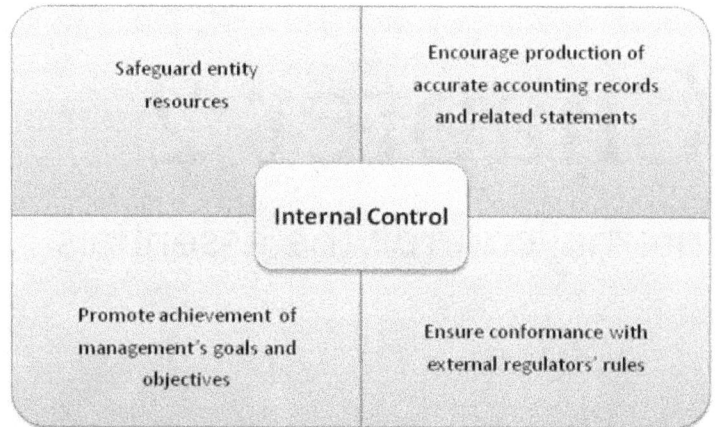

For the purpose of this discussion about the objectives of internal controls, let's imagine ourselves working in a mid-sized not-for-profit hospital, Moapa Memorial Hospital (MMH).

STOP. Pair up with a classmate and work on the following assignment. Using the objectives listed in Exhibit 2.1, identify a few realistic examples for each objective for MMH (to get you started, I provided one for each objective). Create a two-column table like the one shown below into which you'll write your ideas.

Internal control objective	Examples
Safeguard entity resources	Securing drugs and medical supplies kept in the Emergency Room
Encourage production of accurate accounting records and related financial statements	Reviewing uncollectible receivables monthly and writing off as necessary
Promote achievement of management's goals and objectives	Tracking unplanned readmission rates and comparing to management's expectations
Ensure conformance with external regulators' rules	Medical waste is disposed of according to relevant municipal, state, and federal laws

Now reflect on what you and your partner wrote. See if your list has similarities with the descriptions below.

---

4   Ibid.

Safeguard entity resources

It's not hard to imagine the broad range of resources in a hospital. These would include current assets like cash, receivables, and medical supplies inventory as well as long-term assets such as property, plant and equipment (PP&E) and investments. MMH certainly would like to protect its resources from theft (for example, cash, laptop computers or drugs from the pharmacy) and misuse (perhaps the laundry facilities, hospital minivan, or Radiology Department imaging equipment). Did you think of these two categories, protecting against asset theft and misuse (or inappropriate use)? Any entity's resources are vulnerable to these two risks. A system of internal control seeks to care for and safeguard entity assets from theft by staffers or outsiders, and misuse by staff and others inside the entity.

Encourage production of accurate accounting records and related financial statements

Who are the users of Moapa Memorial's accounting data and financial statements? The internal user groups would include staffers, management, and the hospital's board of trustees. The Internal Revenue Service, granting foundations, patients, Medicare and Medicaid, and insurance companies would constitute some of the external users. All rely on trustworthy and timely data for their work and decision making. Before the cafeteria manager prepares a purchase requisition for supplies, he wants to know how close he is to reaching his monthly budget for supplies expense. The treasurer requires a listing of projected cash inflows and outflows for the coming quarter. The hospital's trustees need to understand the current debt load before it authorizes issuing bonds for the construction of a new emergency and critical care center. An accounts payable clerk at insurance provider Anthem Blue Cross Blue Shield compares the hospital's invoice for an orthopedic surgical procedure against a list of customary and usual charges before she authorizes reimbursement to MMH. The Moapa Community Foundation reviews MMH's last five years' financial statements as part of the evaluation process for a grant application received from the hospital. Moapa Memorial's system of internal control must include policies and practices that support accurate data gathering, processing, storage, and communication, thereby increasing the confidence of those using its accounting information system's data.

Promote achievement of management's goals and objectives

How can managers determine if their short-term or long-range objectives and goals are being met? Consider the information needs of three hospital managers. A nursing manager at the Moapa Cancer Center must develop next month's staff work schedules while staying within the salary budget. An assistant manager from the hospital's Human Resources Department wants to measure the impact of the new flex-time policy on hourly-paid staffers. And the MMH vice president for operations would like to know if average discharge times have decreased following implementation of new steps to streamline and coordinate the patient discharge process. Accessing both financial and non-financial data, managers can see whether they are meeting, exceeding, or failing to reach various financial or operational targets. Working with data that faithfully represents the hospital's transactions helps to promote reliable assessment and decision making by these managers.

Ensure conformance with external regulators' rules

Can you imagine the number of private and public regulators that review or govern the daily operations of a hospital? MMH needs to comply with the requirements and regulations of municipal, state, federal, and industry bodies. Think about some of these: the chief financial officer needs to send the hospital's Form 990 to the Internal Revenue Service by the filing deadline to avoid penalties. Incidences of infectious diseases must be reported to the county and state health departments as well as the Centers for Disease Control and Prevention in Atlanta. The hospital's housekeeping department has to follow state and federal EPA (Environmental Protection Agency) regulations for proper disposal of hazardous waste products. Failure to conform to these external entities' rules can result in the imposition of penalties, fines, and warning notices. The hospital would like to limit the amount of negative publicity associated with these actions as well as the financial impact of penalties and fines. Creating a reliable collection of practices to ensure the hospital complies with regulators' rules and policies is the focus of this internal control objective.

We might have used a government agency, or a merchandiser, manufacturer, or service entity for this discussion about internal control objectives. Make no mistake: regardless of the form and structure of the entity, the objectives of a system of internal control are the same. A school, an engineering firm, a sporting goods retailer, and the Gallatin County government all want to see that their assets are protected, records and financial statements are dependable, and be assured that internal and external procedures are being followed.

In this next section, we will take a short journey back in time and introduce several of the instrumental pronouncements that influence the way businesses think about internal control.

Chapter Core Question 2: What are some of the noteworthy pronouncements contributing to current ideas about internal control?

Influential Sources on Internal Control

The COSO Report–1992

Nearly 20 years ago, the Committee of Sponsoring Organizations (American Accounting Association, American Institute of CPAs, Institute of Management Accountants, Financial Executives International, and Institute of Internal Auditors) published a monumental report on the components of internal control. While not mandatory that its framework be adopted, Internal Control – Integrated Framework emerged as the *de facto* set of practices for internal control in business entities. The COSO Report – as it came to be called – has influenced accountants and auditors for a generation. Accounting information systems and auditing textbooks commonly include coverage of the COSO Framework, a methodology used to

Exhibit 2.2 – Components of internal control

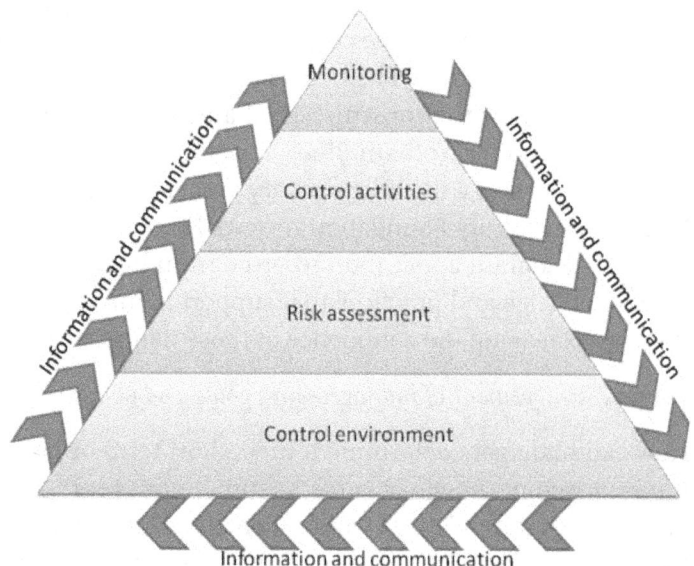

assess and design systems of internal control. You can read the executive summary of the COSO Report at the COSO Web site (http://www.coso.org/IC-IntegratedFramework-summary.htm).

Let's examine the COSO Framework's fundamental five components of internal control: the control environment; risk assessment, control activities, monitoring, and information and communication.

The COSO Report uses a pyramid to graphically depict the relationship of the five internal control components. Later versions of the COSO Integrated Framework incorporate a three-dimensional cube and include the objectives of internal control as well as operating units to illustrate an expanded view of the significance of internal control. As we are introducing the report and the components in this chapter, however, I will use the original pyramid-shaped image to offer visual support for our discussion. It also lends credence to the concept that these components build on, or support each other in somewhat of a hierarchy – something that is missing in the cube version of the graphic.

Control Environment

The control environment at Satyam certainly seems to have been very poor, didn't it? Its chairman, Mr. Raju, was able to alter the financial statements and create cash balances that had no basis in reality. How was this possible?

The control environment is the underpinning for the other four internal control components. Situated at the bottom of the pyramid, a strong control environment serves as the foundation for a solid system of internal control. The internal control attitudes of every member of the entity are influenced by the words and actions of the entity's leaders and managers. Take a look at what is written about the control environment in the COSO Report:

"Control environment factors include the integrity, ethical values and competence of the entity's people; management's philosophy and operating style; the way management assigns authority and responsibility, and organizes and develops its people; and the attention and direction provided by the board of directors."[5]

If an entity's executives don't give much consideration to characteristics like integrity and competence, such attitudes may easily trickle down and across to everyone affiliated with the entity. Soon, a "who cares" or "so what" climate emerges; practices created to protect resources and advance the creation of accurate financial records and reporting lose their effectiveness.

Risk Assessment

Satyam, not unlike other computer services companies, faced a number of business risks related to a dynamic and highly competitive global business atmosphere. These risks had a clear and direct impact on Satyam's financial results. Clients outsourcing their IT operations were scaling back these activities given the global recession and a need to curb operating expenses. Facing a potential decrease of revenues, Raju faced pressures from various sources causing him to overstate Satyam's revenues and cash position.

The process of evaluating internal control efficacy and creating internal controls requires that we understand the internal and external risks that can threaten the entity. The COSO Report states:

"Risk assessment is the identification and analysis of relevant risks to achievement of the objectives [business objectives], forming a basis for determining how the risks should be managed."[6]

If an entity demonstrates a strong control environment, it raises the likelihood that its leaders and managers will recognize and acknowledge these business risks, then directly address their impact with responsible and ethical actions. A genuine belief in the value added by strong controls promotes awareness of business hot spots and receptiveness to doing what's necessary to mitigate them.

Control Activities

Even among entities that understand the significance of a solid control environment, deterring, detecting, and reducing the impact of business risks and threats is a challenging task. Now imagine how much more difficult it would be in the absence of policies and procedures aimed at standardizing business practices and accounting transaction processing. News articles don't offer many details about the degree of control activities in place at Satyam Computer Services. We don't know whether the external auditors assessed the internal controls to be strong, observed a few minor weaknesses, or completely missed the warning flags of chronic internal control problems.

Consider the language used in the COSO Report to talk about internal control activities:

5   Committee of Sponsoring Organizations. 1992. *Internal Control – Integrated Framework*. New York.

6   Ibid.

"Control activities occur throughout the organization, at all levels and in all functions. They include a range of activities as diverse as approvals, authorizations, verifications, reconciliations, reviews of operating performance, security of assets and segregation of duties."[7]

These activities will be visited in detail in a subsequent section of this chapter and throughout the textbook. Control activities comprise a core characteristic of the approach used in this textbook.

Monitoring

"Internal control systems need to be monitored—a process that assesses the quality of the system's performance over time. This is accomplished through ongoing monitoring activities, separate evaluations or a combination of the two."[8]

Once internal controls are put into place, they need to be periodically reviewed for effectiveness. If found to be ineffective, they are evaluated, modified, implemented, and subsequently reviewed. Sometimes internal and external events will trigger the need to reassess business risks and an entity's internal controls. The worst manner in which to handle internal controls is to ignore them after they have been adopted. Entities might take an "if it isn't broken, don't fix it" attitude about internal control activities; yet we know from experience and the many publicized cases of accounting and financial statement fraud that this is a dangerous posture to take.

Information and Communication

How important is the component *information and communication* to a system of internal control? Concise paraphrasing cannot replace the description from the COSO Report.

"Information systems produce reports, containing operational, financial and compliance-related information, that make it possible to run and control the business. They deal not only with internally generated data, but also information about external events, activities and conditions necessary to informed business decision-making and external reporting. Effective communication also must occur in a broader sense, flowing down, across and up the organization. All personnel must receive a clear message from top management that control responsibilities must be taken seriously. They must understand their own role in the internal control system, as well as how individual activities relate to the work of others. They must have a means of communicating significant information upstream. There also needs to be effective communication with external parties, such as customers, suppliers, regulators and shareholders."[9]

Barrier-free information and communication flows are what link the control environment to risk assessment, risk assessment to control activities, and control activities to monitoring. In the absence of open vertical and horizontal communication channels, a system of internal control can suffer because of gaps between ideas and practices, or philosophy and implementation. Evaluating, designing, introducing, and ongoing monitoring of internal controls will be affected if information and communication are incomplete, inaccurate, or stymied.

To conclude, the COSO Report's Internal Control Framework is considered to be one of the key sources of guidance to create and sustain a durable system of internal control.

The Sarbanes-Oxley Act of 2002

In the aftermath of the financial accounting scandals of Enron, WorldCom, Adelphia Communications, HealthSouth, and other corporations, Congress enacted a law with widespread effects on the financial reporting

---

7   Ibid.

8   Ibid.

9   Ibid.

activities of business and not-for-profit entities. The Sarbanes-Oxley Act of 2002, signed into law by then-President George W. Bush on July 30, 2002, includes several sections central to internal control practices. You need to be acquainted with two sections of the Act, Section 302 and Section 404 (the Act can be viewed at http://www.gpo.gov/fdsys/pkg/PLAW-107publ204/pdf/PLAW-107publ204.pdf).

Section 302 of the Sarbanes-Oxley Act of 2002 focuses on the duty of the chief executive officer and chief financial officer to certify that they: (a) have read the reports; (b) are unaware of major misstatements in the reports; (c) believe the reports accurately depict the entity's financial condition and performance; (d) are ultimately responsible for the internal control system; (e) have disclosed significant problems with the internal control system; and (f) identified key changes to the internal controls subsequent to the date of their review. These certifications are required for each quarterly and annual report (SEC Form 10-Q and 10-K) issued by the entity.

Section 404 of the Act, though only 20 lines in length, created great tumult and confusion among public accountants and their clients in the first few years after its enactment. The law states that publicly traded companies filing their annual reports with the Securities and Exchange Commission must include a management report indicating management is responsible "for establishing and maintaining an adequate internal control structure and procedures for financial reporting"[10]. This report also includes a statement from management assessing the entity's financial reporting internal controls.

External auditors get involved in the game, too, and the span of a typical audit was broadened to include the auditor's evaluation of management's assertions about internal controls over financial reporting. As a result of these requirements of Section 404, corporations restructured their internal audit departments and designed new internal control assessment procedures for financial reporting controls. Public accounting firms providing audit services also reorganized how their services would be delivered in light of these mandatory evaluative measures.

Some believe the additional assessments and evaluations have helped reduce the number of financial reporting fraud incidents in the last decade. Others claim financial statement misstatements and fraud continue to take place, but in the years since the effective date of the Act there have not been the high-profile failures and frauds that first captured the attention of businesspeople and lawmakers as did those in the last quarter of 2001.

Statement on Auditing Standards No. 109 – 2006

The AICPA, in SAS 109 (now identified as AU Section 314[11]), describes fieldwork standards to which auditors should adhere. AU Sections 314.40 through 314.101 specifically refer to the COSO Report's Internal Control Framework in the discussion of appropriate steps that should be adopted in an audit. Additionally, AU Section 314.47 reinforces the importance of COSO guidance by incorporating content from another COSO document, Enterprise Risk Management – Integrated Framework, published in 2004. The multidimensional enterprise risk management matrix (the "cube" mentioned earlier in the chapter) is used to help auditors understand the interrelatedness of an entity's objectives and associated internal control activities.

These three documents (COSO Report, Sarbanes-Oxley Act of 2002, and SAS 109/AU Section 314) are a representative sample of how the subject of internal control permeates accounting and auditing. Now let's turn to the last section of this chapter and take a look an internal control toolkit you can use to evaluate, design, and implement internal controls in any entity.

---

10   Sarbanes-Oxley Act of 2002. P.L. 107-204. 116 STAT 745. Available at: http://www.gpo.gov/fdsys/pkg/PLAW-107publ204/pdf/PLAW-107publ204.pdf.

11   AU Section 314. 2006. New York: AICPA. Available at: http://www.aicpa.org/research/standards/auditattest/downloadabledocuments/au-00314.pdf

Chapter Core Question 3: What is the ASSRAV internal control toolkit and how is it used?

ASSRAV – the Internal Control Toolkit

You get home from work on a Thursday evening. After changing out of your suit and tight shoes and into a comfortable pair of jeans and socks, you wander into the kitchen to prepare dinner. Gathering some fresh asparagus from the refrigerator and an avocado from a basket on your kitchen counter, you place them near the sink to rinse. But not long after you turn on the water you notice the water is not quickly flowing down the drain. Rather, the water is pooling in the sink. You try a couple of ways to deal with the blockage but nothing seems to make a difference. Since you are having guests over for dinner tomorrow evening, you decide it's best to call a plumber now to come over and clear the drain.

Fortunately for you it's a slow night and the plumber arrives at your apartment within the hour. He opens his toolbox and pulls out a plumber's snake, a special tool used to auger through a drainpipe and break through blockages. After a bit of work, you hear water running swiftly and smoothly down the drain. The plumber gives you a bill and takes his leave.

Let's reflect on this scenario: among all of the tools in his toolbox, why did he opt for the plumber's snake? He chose it because it was the most appropriate tool for the situation. He probably had several hammers, screwdrivers, pipe wrenches, socket wrenches, and other tools from which to pick. But he evaluated the problem, selected the best means to deal with the problem, and went to work. If his tool of first choice didn't work, he likely would have reassessed the problem and the tools available to him before deciding on another course of action with a different tool.

This is not unlike what happens when an entity faces threats, weaknesses, or vulnerabilities and needs to develop internal control activities to lessen such risks. Recall the description of internal control (in Chapter 1 and the opening pages of this chapter): a system of internal control is a collection of people, policies, and practices working together to protect resources, improve accounting recordkeeping, and ensure compliance with internal and external objectives, goals, and regulations. Internal controls (called internal control activities in the COSO Framework) are the tools used to accomplish the internal control objectives. Just as the plumber carries a toolbox with different tools

Exhibit 2.3 – ASSRAV: your internal control toolkit

A	uthorization
S	upervision
S	eparation of duties
R	ecords and documents
A	sset access restrictions
V	erification (independent)

for different jobs, so too will you "carry" an internal control toolkit outfitted with six tools to support the work of designing internal controls to tackle business risks. Exhibit 2.3 identifies the tools in your **ASSRAV** toolkit. The remainder of this chapter discusses how to use these tools to lessen the impact of various business risks.

Consider the Moapa Memorial Hospital examples from earlier in this chapter. We'll use these to demonstrate how the tools in your ASSRAV toolkit can be used to design cost effective internal controls for the hospital.

Authorization

As described in the first section of this chapter, Moapa Memorial Hospital has a number of assets it would like to protect. One internal control tool in your toolkit is authorization: obtaining approval or permission from someone to do or access something. Consider the hospital's pharmacy. The nature of controlled substances (prescription drugs) requires that they be safeguarded against theft or misuse. Can you think of some risks related to the drugs stored in the pharmacy? Probably the most significant threat comes from hospital staff removing painkillers for their own use – or to illegally sell.

Suppose a nurse from the emergency room is working with a patient suffering from kidney stones. The ER doctor prescribes two narcotics to relieve some of the pain and make the patient drowsy while awaiting the stones' passage. The ER nurse goes to the pharmacy to retrieve these drugs. To discourage or deter the nurse from picking the drugs himself, MMH should have an internal control in place that requires the pharmacist to have a doctor's written or electronic authorization before she releases the drugs to the nurse. Could a nurse create an order and forge a doctor's signature? Of course it's possible. Recall that internal controls can never stop fraud or theft and misuse of assets. But if the pharmacist reviews the written or electronic prescription request and asks a few questions of the nurse, a large percentage of threats can be reduced.

Supervision

Sometimes the mere presence of monitoring equipment or people responsible for overseeing work serves to sufficiently deter theft and misuse of assets. That's the purpose of the ASSRAV tool we call supervision. Reviewing, watching, or monitoring the tasks and behaviors of others can discourage attempts by staffers, patients, visitors, and vendors from stealing or inappropriately using hospital resources.

The cashier in the hospital gift shop or cafeteria is in a position that easily allows him access to cash. It's not practical to position a supervisor or manager to constantly watch that the cashier doesn't steal cash from the register. Instead, a cost-effective supervision technique is to install an overhead video camera pointing at the cashier and register. The likelihood is low that cashiers and visitors would take cash from the register knowing there's a camera recording their actions.

Separation of duties

The third tool in your ASSRAV toolkit, separation of duties, distributes or allocates the parts of a task or activity among different people. Seems unnecessary and inefficient, doesn't it? Let's imagine the following situation at Moapa Memorial Hospital.

A clerk in the billing department entered data about procedures performed, drugs administered, and therapeutic services delivered to an orthopedic patient who stayed in the hospital for five days. The patient's insurance company reimbursed the hospital for a small percentage of these costs. The patient, who earns a small income and doesn't have many personal assets, visits the billing department to explain that she cannot afford to pay the part of the hospital charges not covered by insurance.

What happens now? Can the clerk simply write off the uncollectible balance of the patient's account receivable? Well, she could, but such action could set a precedent that the hospital's financial executives would not want to sustain. Once word spread throughout the region that the hospital will write off your balance owed if you ask, patients from near and far would flock to the hospital for treatment – and subsequent payment reductions! Clearly this is not a desirable outcome.

A separation of duties attempts to decentralize three key tasks: (a) recordkeeping; (b) authorization; and (c) custody (access) to assets. If practical, these tasks should be handled by different people. When it's not possible to do this, the entity should strive to divide recordkeeping and authorization among different staffers. MMH would want to separate the recordkeeping and authorization tasks related to A/R write-offs by having the billing clerk take charge of recordkeeping (updating the patient A/R files) but assigning the review and authorization of the write-off to a credit manager or other financial/business manager at the hospital.

Records and documents

A maternity patient has been admitted to the hospital and will deliver her baby within the day. To properly account for the cost of services for the woman and her newborn, MMH's billing department gathers documentation (evidence) from the departments providing services to the woman and her newborn. These might be paper-based or digital orders and receipts. During pre-admission procedures conducted weeks before the birth of the baby, the hospital would have collected the woman's personal information and insurance provider details. The data in her patient billing record would be supported by tangible evidence showing the reasons for the fees and their calculations.

Why do we emphasize the importance of records and documentation? Without this evidence, we cannot determine the accuracy of the amounts billed to insurance companies and patients. Nor is it possible to trace amounts reported on the hospital's financial statements to the source documents used to initiate requests for procedures, medications, and supplies. Physician and hospital productivity cannot be properly evaluated. Your ASSRAV tool – records and documents – offers justification for the quantities and dollar amounts entered into an entity's journals, ledgers, and databases, and which subsequently are used to produce the financial statements.

Asset access restrictions

Moapa Memorial Hospital has numerous assets it must protect. These range from maintenance supplies to controlled substances, IT devices to surgical equipment. Can you think of an asset the hospital wishes to safeguard and develop an internal control that would restrict access to that asset? What is it?

We can imagine the hospital would want to limit access to the operating rooms. But who should have access? The obvious people would include surgeons, surgical nurses, and anesthesiologists; but housekeeping and maintenance need admission as well as technicians. So how can the hospital limit access only to those whose work requires them to have permission?

One technique is to install a card reader or biometric scanner that can be used in combination with or without a numeric keypad. When a surgical nurse wants to enter one of the operating rooms, she scans her ID badge (encoded with a bar code, magnetic strip, or smart chip) and enters a password or PIN using the numeric keypad. The database would match her identification against a list of places in the hospital where she has permission to gain entrance. She would be allowed to enter the area. Those lacking authorization would be denied admission.

Verification (independent)

Your final tool in the ASSRAV toolkit looks to people and entities outside of the business process to play a role in a system of internal control. Let's illustrate by asking a question. What documents would you want to have if you were one of the accounts payable clerks at MMH responsible for paying vendor invoices?

STOP. Find a classmate and make a list of those documents. When you're done, read on.

As you'll learn in Chapter 6, entities paying their vendor invoices match the data and dollar amounts on the invoices against the data shown on the following documents:

- purchase requisition (prepared by the staffer who wants to purchase something)

- purchase order (prepared by the purchasing department or a designated staffer in the requesting department)

- receiving report (prepared by the department that receives the delivered goods)

The first two documents are prepared by staffers who have a relationship with the purchase, so they are not independent of the purchasing process. But the receiving clerk has no connection to the purchase. He neither requested nor placed the order. His role is merely to receive the box or package when it arrives and deliver it to the requisitioner. To enhance the nature of such independent verification, the receiving department typically gets a copy of the purchase order without the order quantity or prices – what we call the *blind copy* of the purchase order. It forces the receiving clerk to independently count and verify the goods received. The receiving clerk prepares his receiving report, which is forwarded to the accounts payable office and used by the payables clerk to reconcile what was ordered with what was delivered and invoiced by the vendor.

Some Final Thoughts on Internal Control

The goal of this chapter is to introduce fundamental concepts and related knowledge in the area of internal control. For all of the benefits yielded by a solid internal control system, such systems cannot always stop fraud or the theft and misuse of assets when someone is possessed by a deep and strong motivation and ability to commit these acts. What we hope to accomplish is to alter individual behavior and deter (discourage), detect, and limit losses that have occurred. Why can't we prevent or stop the risks?

One of the guidelines in designing systems of internal control is a philosophy people apply in their daily lives: the cost-benefit principle. When deciding among alternative courses of action we generally make choices that minimize the cost of what we give up and maximize the benefit obtained. We wouldn't spend more money to implement an internal control than the value of the resource we are trying to safeguard. Would-be fraudsters who understand this constraint are always on the lookout for opportunities, no matter how insignificant. What we today refer to as the Fraud Triangle was in fact developed nearly 70 years ago by criminologist Donald Cressey. He concluded that pressure and rationalization – in addition to opportunity – are the motivators for committing fraud[12]. In 2004, Wolfe and Hermanson expanded Cressey's approach, emphasizing an additional dimension to explain what might lead a person to fraud: the capability to carry out the financial statement manipulation or theft or misuse of resources.[13]

In designing and evaluating internal controls it is essential that you think like someone who intends to commit fraud or misuse and steal assets. Small cracks and gaps (opportunities) evident in daily tasks and business processes can be exploited by a strongly motivated and capable individual. Occasions for fraud, misuse, and theft must be identified, after which controls can be adopted to discourage these behaviors and make the path difficult for the dishonest person.

Internal controls (control activities, as defined in the COSO Framework) address both financial and non-financial dimensions of an entity. Of course it's important to develop controls that will protect assets and help generate reliable accounting records. But if you consider the third and fourth objectives of a system of internal control – ensuring compliance with management's goals and adhering to external organizations' regulations – internal controls also include those of an operational nature.

> **Internal controls benefit governmental agencies, for-profit entities, and not-for-profit organizations.**

Even for entities not subject to Section 404 of the Sarbanes-Oxley Act, having a strong system of internal control is a best practice that cannot be overlooked. No matter how small the entity, internal controls will be enhanced if authorization, recordkeeping, and custody can be separated. Not-for-profit entities and government agencies

---

12   Wells, J. T. (1997). *Occupational Fraud and Abuse*. Austin, TX: Obsidian Publishing Company, p. 11.

13   Wolfe, D. and D. Hermanson (2004). The Fraud Diamond: Considering the Four Elements of Fraud, *The CPA Journal*, December (Vol. 74, Issue 12), 38-41.

are also in the fight against fraud and asset misuse, and promote efficient and effective daily operations by adapting elements of Section 404 to their environments.

Internal control is a critical subject in the study and practice of accounting information systems. You will observe some applications of it in our next chapter. The topic of flowcharting – documenting the steps in an activity or process – incorporates a few internal control examples.

Chapter Core Vocabulary

ASSRAV – stands for authorization, supervision, separation of duties, records and documentation, restricting asset access, and verification. It is a collection of practices that can strengthen an entity's system of internal control.

Best practices – the ways that tasks or processes are performed to consistently yield high results or performance. Industry-leading entities generally set best practices that others follow.

Control activities – practices and procedures used to achieve the objectives of a system of internal control.

Control environment – an entity's beliefs, attitudes, and actions toward a system of internal control. It is affected by the highest level of executives and leaders, whose behaviors tickle down the entity hierarchy and influence the internal control behaviors of other managers and non-management staff.

Information and communication –communicating information about internal control risks and practices is necessary so an entity's staff and management understand how and why internal control activities are being created. Awareness of one's role in a system of internal control can improve how internal controls are viewed by staffers and management.

Internal control – a collection of people, policies, and practices that (a) safeguard entity resources, (b) encourage production of accurate accounting records and related financial statements, (c) promote achievement of management's goals and objectives, and (d) ensure conformance with external regulators' rules.

Monitoring – after internal controls are implemented they need to be occasionally reviewed for effectiveness. If found ineffective, they are re-evaluated, modified, implemented, and subsequently reviewed.

Risk assessment – identifying and analyzing the relevant risks to achieving an entity's objectives, and once identified, establishing basic principles for managing the risks.

Chapter 3

Documentation: basic flowcharting skills

Chapter Core Questions

1. What is a physical data flow diagram and how do I prepare one?

2. What is a document flowchart and how do I create one?

Introduction

You work as an auditor in the internal audit department at Pasta Valley, a chain of Italian restaurants in the Pacific Northwest. During the third quarter of the fiscal year the corporate internal audit staff is responsible for conducting various internal control reviews. You've been assigned to the team reviewing the payroll process. Your portion of the work involves administering internal control questionnaires and conducting interviews with restaurant managers and staff in a seven-county region in Idaho and Oregon. Before you start your weeklong road trip to visit these sites you decide to familiarize yourself with the timekeeping and payroll process since you haven't been assigned to any audit work with the payroll process during your three year employment with Pasta Valley. What's the best way to accomplish this?

I don't know about you, but I'd quickly lose interest in learning about the process if I had to read page after page of narrative describing how staff record their hours worked, restaurant managers review and approve bi-weekly payroll, and corporate accounting staff process paychecks. Would it make more sense to see a graphic representation – perhaps a diagram – to grasp a basic understanding of the steps in the process? Yes, it should be more efficient and effective than navigating through thousands of words.

This chapter introduces the fundamental concepts of flowcharting and shows how to draw two of the more common accounting flowcharts: the physical data flow diagram and the document flowchart. Each will be described and illustrated. As well, there are opportunities to draw a few charts yourself. First, we'll turn our focus to the physical data flow diagram.

Chapter Core Question 1: What is a physical data flow diagram and how do I prepare one?

Physical Data Flow Diagram

The **physical data flow diagram** shows data sources (inputs), actions performed on the data (processing), and the processed data (outputs). It describes *how* data moves through a business process or activity (one part of a process) and the *entities* (departments, offices, or people) involved in creating, updating, and using this data. Data flow diagrams (DFD) are helpful tools when you want to casually present ideas about activities, processes, or internal controls, not unlike the way accountants and auditors use T-accounts to analyze the impact of accounting transactions.

Exhibit 3.1 – Physical data flow diagram symbol set

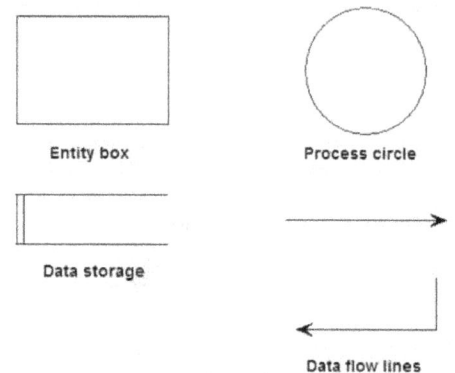

Entity box   Process circle

Data storage   Data flow lines

The data flow diagrams we create will be simple, high-level flowcharts whose intent is to give a general depiction of the steps in a process or activity. What does a DFD look like? Open your favorite Web browser to Google™ images (http://images.google.com/). Now type "physical data flow diagram" in the search box. Examine the first 18 or 20 images that appear on your screen. Pretty diverse, yes? Seems like there's no standardization or agreement on the shapes (icons or symbols) used, right? Welcome to the world of work! Each entity generally has its preferences for the drawing guidelines and symbols used to prepare a DFD. But to ease your burden, we will use only the four icons shown in Exhibit 3.1.

The best way to learn how to do something is to try it yourself. So let's get started drawing your first data flow diagram.

Drawing a Physical Data Flow Diagram

STOP. Find a partner or two with whom to work. List in order of occurrence, the steps taken in the revenue cycle activity that follows. After you identify them we'll narrow down the steps to those that document the activity and affect the accounting system. Then you'll draw your DFD.

Description of the activity: with a two hour break between classes, a university student walks into the HK Donuts shop across the street from campus. He orders a cup of coffee and a lentil curry croquette, and uses his debit card to pay for the items.

Please don't read on until you and your partners have listed what you believe to be the sequence of steps followed in this business activity.

Suggested list of steps for this revenue cycle sales activity:

1.   Student decides what he'd like to eat and drink.

2.   Student orders items from sales clerk.

3.   Sales clerk enters customer order into the retail POS (point-of-sale) system.

4.   Student hands his debit card to sales clerk.

5.   Sales clerk swipes debit card through card reader and enters dollar amount of the sale on card reader keypad.

6.   Student's bank determines whether his account balance has sufficient funds to cover the payment.

7.   Sales clerk receives authorization from student's bank.

8.   Sales clerk returns debit card to student along with sales receipt printed by retail POS system.

9.   Sales clerk prepares food and beverage, places on a tray, and gives to student.

10. Student searches for a comfortable seat next to the window, sits down, opens his geology textbook, and begins to read, eat, and drink.

Narrow down the steps

Only those steps that document the activity and impact the accounting records of the entity are included in the physical data flow diagram. Which steps don't alter HK Donuts' accounting records or provide evidence (documentation) of the transaction? They are steps 1, 2, 9, and 10. Choices leading up to the student's decision about what to buy are not recordable events for HK Donuts and can be omitted from the DFD. The sales clerk's gathering of the croquette and coffee and the student's action to select a seat and consume his food and beverage also do not change the accounting records at HK Donuts. Remember, sales revenue, cash, cost of goods sold, and inventory automatically are recorded in Steps 3 and 8.

Steps 3 through 8 should be used to create your data flow diagram. STOP. Get together with your partner(s) and using the symbols in Exhibit 3.1 please draw your first DFD. Don't look ahead to Exhibit 3.2 until you finished drawing!

Exhibit 3.2 – Suggested Data Flow Diagram for HK Donuts' Sales Process

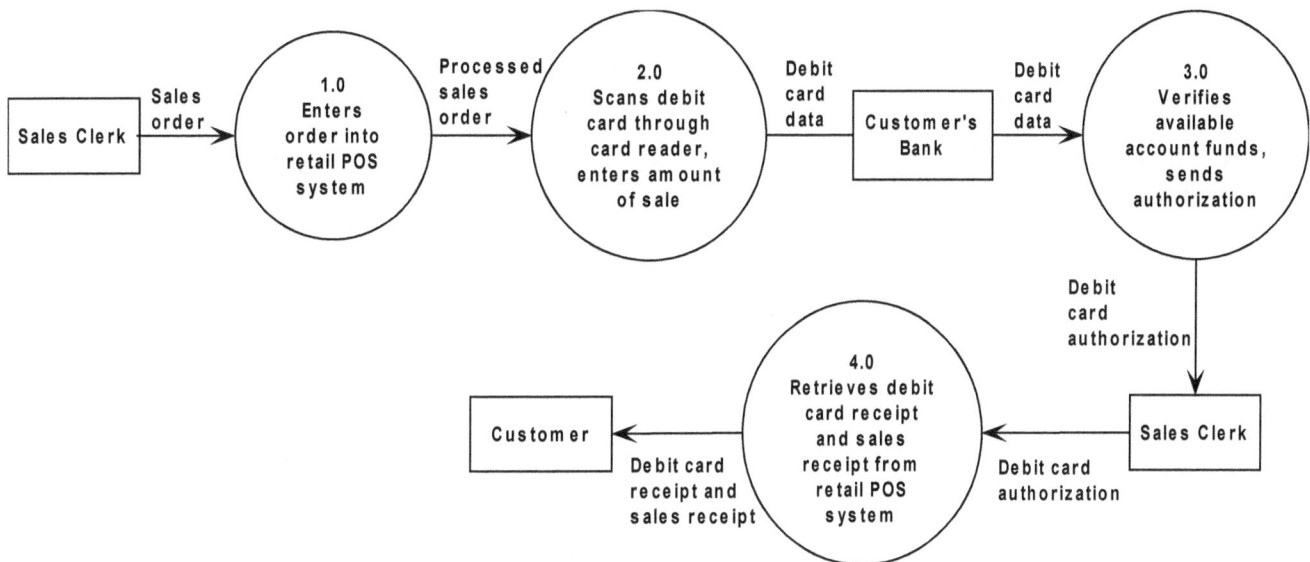

Does your flowchart look something like this? Congratulations, you've successfully created your first physical data flow diagram. It wasn't that difficult, was it? Imagine you've never been in an HK Donuts shop and don't know about its sales process. After spending just a few minutes with the DFD you can acquire a fairly clear understanding of the sales and cash receipts tasks. While you might feel this is a very simple flowchart, you should develop competence with a straightforward DFD before you tackle the job of flowcharting more complex processes.

STOP. What features do you notice about the HK Donuts data flow diagram? Make a list of the characteristics you observe.

Your list might include the following:

1. The DFD starts and ends with entity boxes.

2. Text inside the box identifies the people involved in the activity. The entity boxes are the *nouns* of your story about business activities.

3. Text inside the circles show the actions performed on the data. The process circles are the *verbs* that give action and movement to your story.

4. Text inside the circles always begins with a verb.

5. Process circles are numbered in sequential order.

6. Flow lines are labeled with the data inputs and outputs. Flow lines to the left of the process circles show the inputs to be processed. Flow lines to the right of the process circles display the processed data (outputs).

7. Flow lines are straight and situated at right angles to the boxes and circles.

8. Flow lines don't cross.

How can a reader of this data flow diagram use it? A new employee at HK Donuts might use the DFD to learn how the sales activity takes place. An accountant or auditor evaluating the effectiveness of the company's internal controls would use the DFD to gain an understanding of the activity and to identify potential internal control weaknesses.

STOP. Now it's time to apply your understanding and skills to draw another data flow diagram. The subject for this DFD will be an expense cycle transaction: paying a vendor invoice. Get your partner and go to work. Here's a brief description of the activity to get you started.

Description of the activity: in today's mail, the accounts payable (A/P) clerk at Mokpo Ceramics receives an invoice from a vendor. One week later she writes a check in payment of the invoice.

First, list the needed steps (in sequential order) to conduct the activity. Please don't read on until you and your partner have listed all the steps in this business activity.

Suggested steps for the expense cycle A/P and cash disbursements activities:

1. Mokpo clerk receives invoice from vendor.

2. Clerk pulls related purchase documents from A/P pending file (purchase order and receiving report).

3. Clerk reviews vendor invoice data and matches with data shown on purchase order and receiving report.

4. Discrepancies, if any, are resolved through conversations with **requisitioner** and/or vendor.

5. Clerk prepares A/P voucher (shows data such as dollar amounts, account numbers to be charged, payment date) and staples invoice, receiving report, and purchase order to the back of the voucher.

6. Clerk schedules invoice for payment and files voucher package in unpaid voucher file by date.

7. On payment date, clerk pulls voucher package from unpaid voucher file.

8. Clerk writes check, but does not sign. *[Why?]*

9. Clerk gives unsigned check and voucher package to authorized check signer (treasurer).

10. Authorized check signer reviews documentation, signs check, and returns all items to A/P clerk.

11. Clerk writes check number and payment date on voucher, mails check and remittance advice to vendor, and files paid voucher in vendor file according to vendor name.

Does your list include these key steps? In the process of comparing your list to the suggested list you might have noted there are a few internal controls embedded in the A/P and cash disbursements activity. Think about your ASSRAV toolkit and see if any of the tools have been employed in this A/P scenario.

Now let's draw the data flow diagram for Mokpo Ceramics' accounts payable activity. When you're finished, examine your DFD and the one shown on the next page. What are the similarities and differences?

Exhibit 3.3 – Mokpo Ceramics DFD for A/P and Cash Disbursements Activities

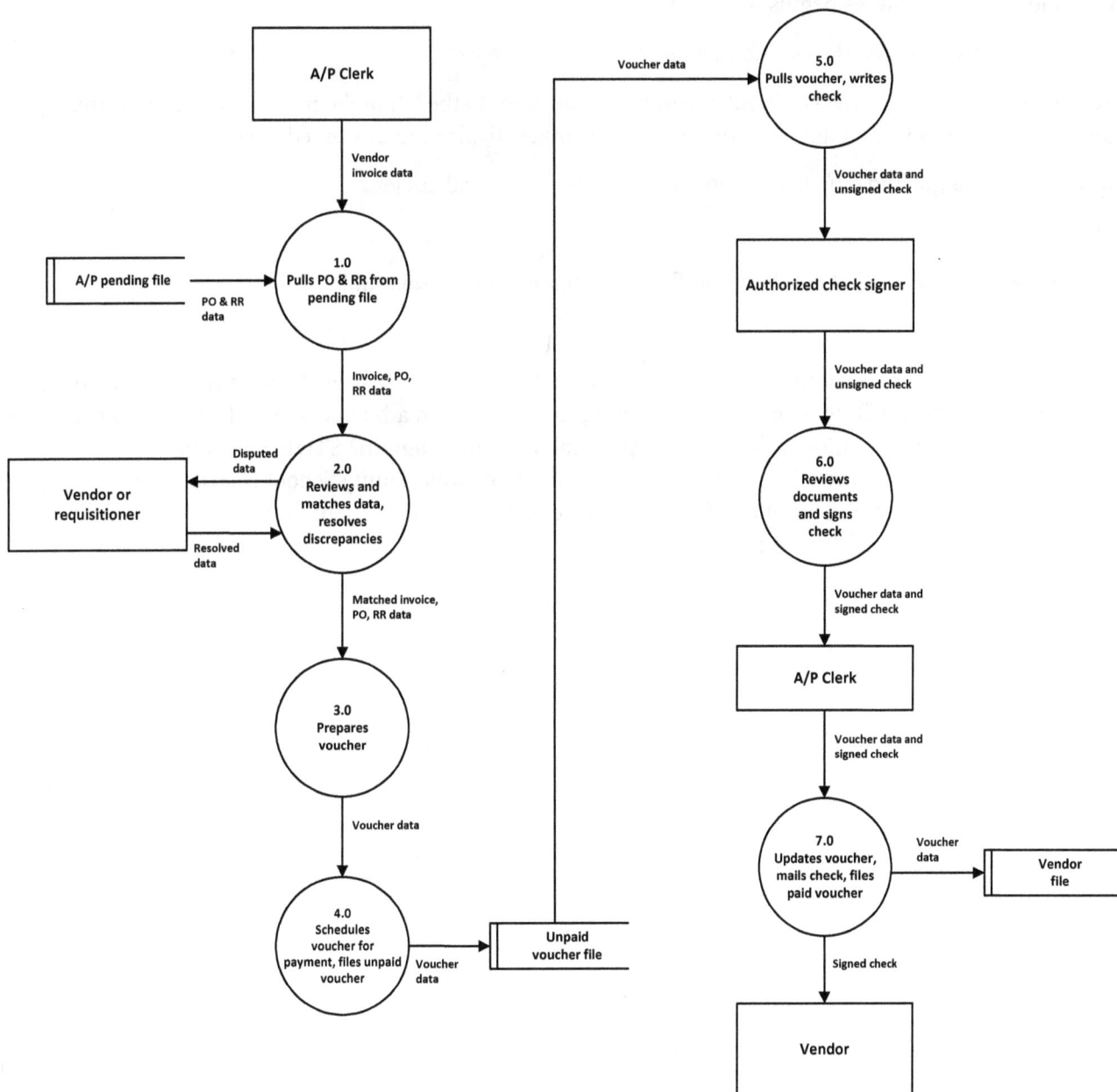

Here you have a more substantial flowchart because the process contains more steps than did the HK Donuts cash sale process. You shouldn't feel intimidated by the length of a flowchart or the number of steps in a business activity or process. My suggestions for drawing flowcharts are not complicated: first, go slow; and second, re-read and revise your flowcharts a few times before you consider them to be finished.

As we wrap up our section on physical data flow diagrams, let's review those general guidelines for creating them.

The DFD starts and ends with entity boxes.

Text inside the box identifies the people involved in the activity. The entity boxes are the *nouns* of your story about business activities.

Text inside the circles show the actions performed on the data. The process circles are the *verbs* that give action and movement to your story.

Text inside the circles always begins with a verb.

Process circles are numbered in sequential order.

Flow lines are labeled with the data input and output. Flow lines to the left of the process circles show the inputs to be processed. Flow lines to the right of the process circles display the processed data.

Flow lines are straight and situated at right angles to the boxes and circles.

Flow lines don't cross.

Chapter Core Question 2: What is a document flowchart and how do I create one?

Document Flowchart

The other type of flowchart commonly used by accountants and auditors is the **document flowchart**. It's used in ways similar to the DFD: to gain an understanding of the steps in a business activity or process. Yet how does this form of documentation differ from the physical data flow diagram? STOP. Find a partner and look at the document flowchart shown in Exhibit 3.4. It depicts the Hopewell County School District's purchasing process. Talk with your partner about the differences you see between a document flowchart and a physical data flow diagram. Make a list of these differences.

Exhibit 3.4 – Hopewell County Schools Purchasing Process

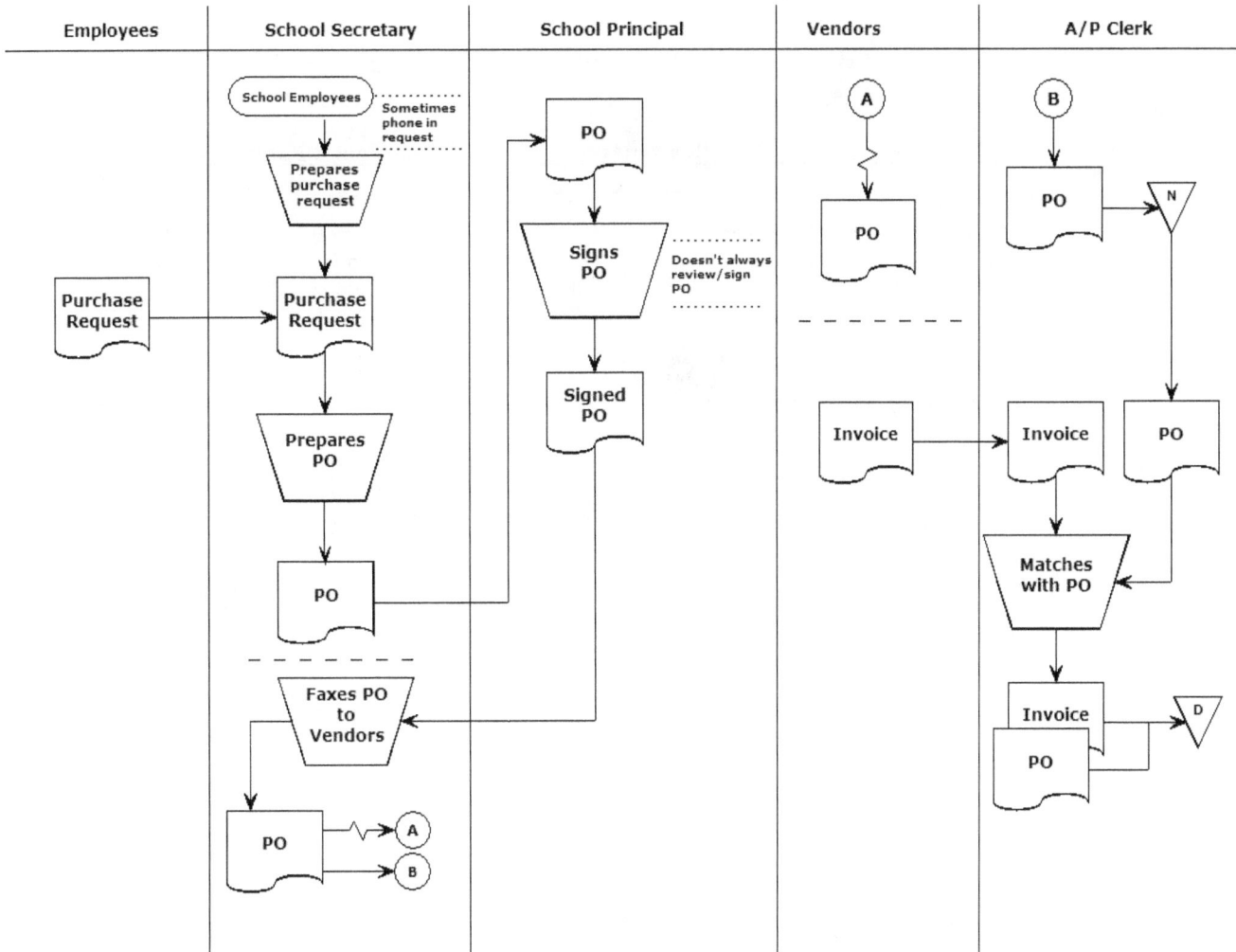

Your list probably includes characteristics such as these:

The document flowchart (DF) is structured using columns to represent the departments or people or entities involved in the business activity or process.

The DF incorporates additional and different symbols than the DFD.

Rectangles and circles have different uses in the DF and the DFD.

Flow lines in the DF have no accompanying data labels.

Good work. Your observations are right on point. Like the data flow diagram, the document flowchart also communicates the steps in an activity or process, but in greater detail and with an emphasis on the documents used and created. You obtain a general knowledge of how something works from reading a DFD. But you really understand the intricacies and details of the activity or process by working with a DF.

Let's see what the HK Donuts cash sales process would look like in a document flowchart. After you've had a chance to study it, we'll compare the DF to the HK Donuts data flow diagram (Exhibit 3.2).

Exhibit 3.5 – HK Donuts Cash Sales Process

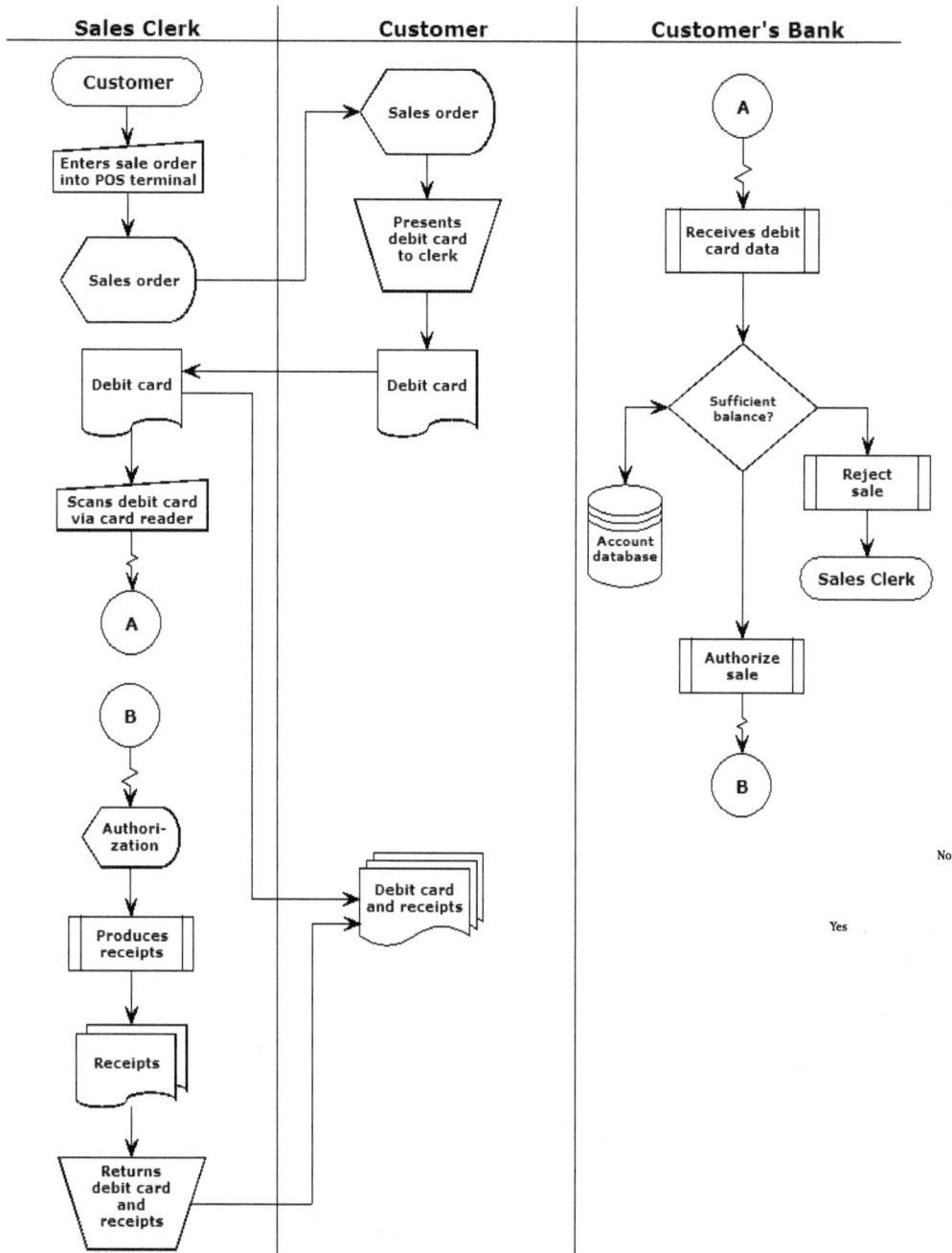

We should pause for a moment and talk about the symbols used in document flowcharts. Others exist, but you'll be introduced to them later.

The **terminator symbol** is misnamed; actually, it shows both the start and end of the document flowchart. Always begin and conclude your DF with terminator symbols.

Physical (manual) actions are depicted by the **manual process symbol**. Stapling source documents together and filing them, verifying data shown on a timecard, matching vendor invoice data against the data on a purchase order and receiving report, collecting cash from a customer all rely on a person's manual effort for performance and not the automatic processes of computer software.

When actions are carried out by application software, the **computerized process symbol** is used instead. Think of the accounts receivable module of an accounting information system updating the customer master file to show receipt of a customer's payment on account; we would depict this action with the computerized process icon instead of the previously described manual process symbol.

The **keyboard/scan data entry symbol** represents data being entered into peripheral devices connected to computers. What kinds of input hardware qualify as peripheral devices? Consider all of the IT components with which we interact and enter data: ATMs, credit/debit card scanners in retail stores, keyboards attached to retail POS systems, desktop PCs, laptops, tablets, smartphones, touch screens on kiosks, biometric scanners in offices, and ID card readers at building or office entrances are just a few of the input devices in daily use.

Exhibit 3.6 – Document flow chart basic symbol set

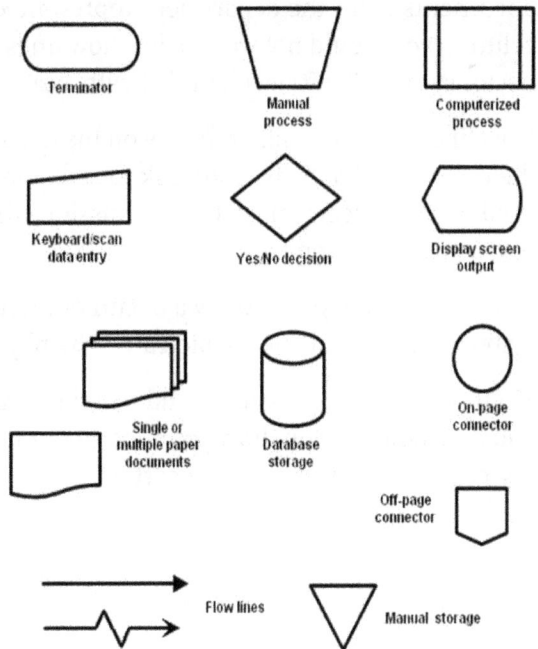

The yes/no **decision symbol** has a distinctive function. At some point in a business activity it might be necessary to ask a closed-ended question (a *yes* or *no* answer is required). If the answer to the question is *yes*, you continue the process with one collection of steps. When the question can be answered with a *no*, you'd take another path through the process. In the HK Donuts document flowchart, the bank needs to determine whether the customer's bank account has enough money to pay for the beverage and food purchase. In the flowchart, we ask the question "is account balance sufficient for payment?". This question is answered in the affirmative or negative.

The keyboard/scan data entry symbol is used to show data being input to a system. After data is processed, it might be output to a **display screen**. Again, reflect on the variety of peripherals in which display screens are embedded: ATMs, credit/debit card scanners, flat screen displays connected to retail POS systems, desktop PCs, laptops, tablets, smartphones, kiosk touch screens, keypads and biometric scanners in offices, and ID card readers at building or office entrances. It's the same collection of peripherals listed in the previous paragraph! These devices can serve as input and output mechanisms. In case you wonder about the shape of the symbol, it is a throwback to the past when computer display terminals looked like huge old-fashioned television sets and were powered by big and thick cathode ray tubes (CRT).

The **document symbol** communicates the business activity's use or production of paper documents. Documents might be the source of data input or they might be created in the output stage. Written timecards serve as the inputs to calculate gross wages; a customer's purchase order is the input to generate a sales order. A paycheck is an output document of the payroll process. The sales invoice is generated from the sales activity. Paper documents can be single- or multiple part forms.

Database storage is used when data is retrieved from or stored to a database rather than paper file storage such as a manila folder, file cabinet, or storage box. Data might be stored temporarily and used later in the process or it could be stored for a while – even permanently archived.

The **connector symbol** is used to show continuation of an activity in another column of the document flowchart. Suppose the activity depicted in the DF has five columns. If you are showing the movement of some paper documents from the department represented in the left-hand column to that represented by the right-hand column, you would not want to use flow lines that cross the width of your flowchart. Instead, you'd insert a connector symbol (typically identified with a capital letter) to indicate where on the flowchart the activity continues.

Flow lines serve a similar purpose on the document flowchart as they do on the data flow diagram: they indicate the direction of activity from task to task. One difference exists with DF flow lines, however. A kinked line is used to show electronic data transmission, such as direct deposit of staff wages or electronic transfers of cash payments and receipts.

Now it's time for you to draw a document flowchart on your own. Refer to the Mokpo Ceramics A/P and cash disbursements activities depicted via the physical data flow diagram in Exhibit 3.3.

STOP. Find a few classmates and together draw a DF for these activities. Rely on Exhibits 3.4 and 3.5 for ideas and assistance as you draw your document flowchart. After you finish, have a look at Exhibit 3.7 on the following pages and compare your chart to it.

Exhibit 3.7 – Suggested document flowchart for Mokpo Ceramics A/P and cash disbursements activities

A/P Clerk	Authorized Check Signer

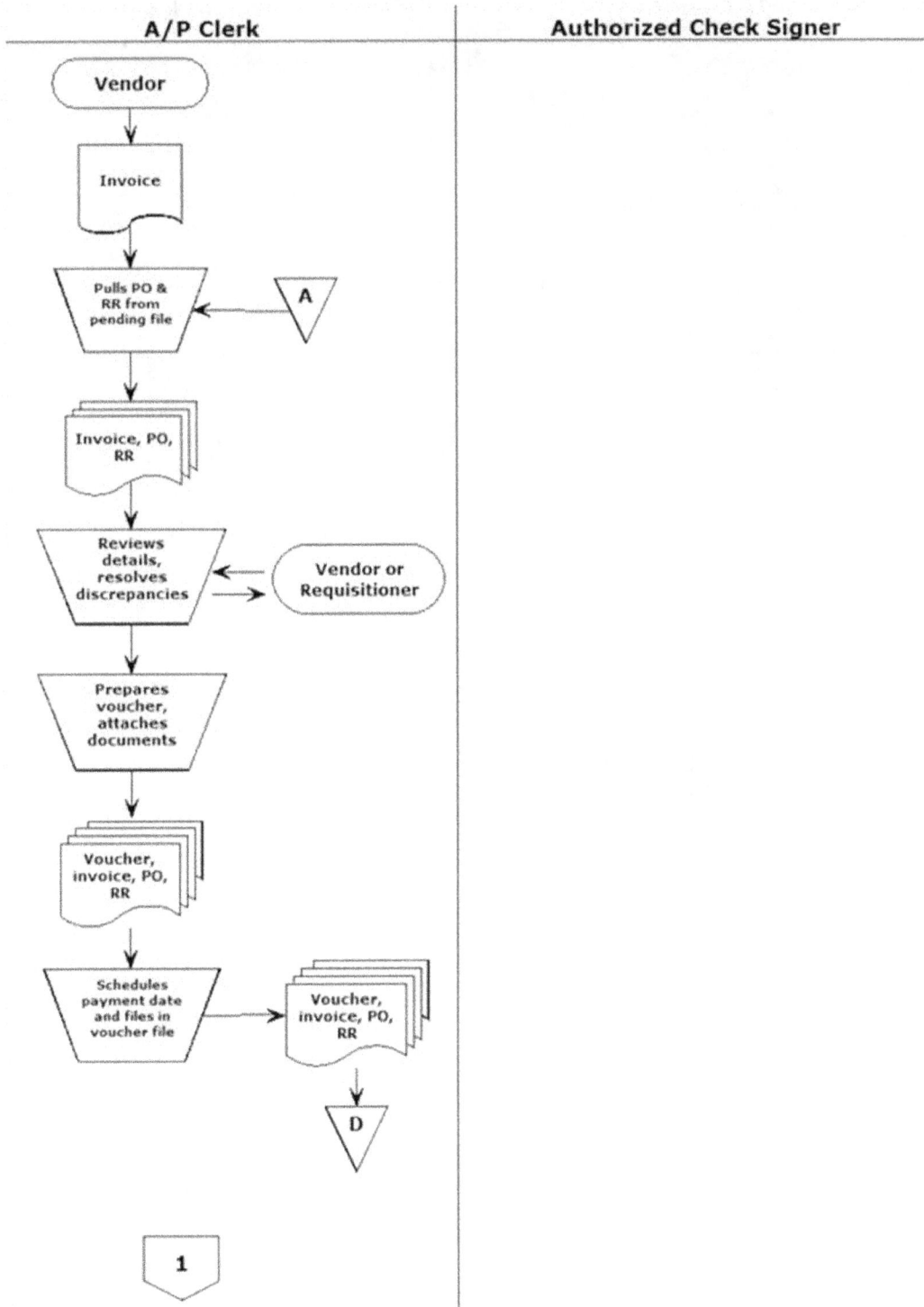

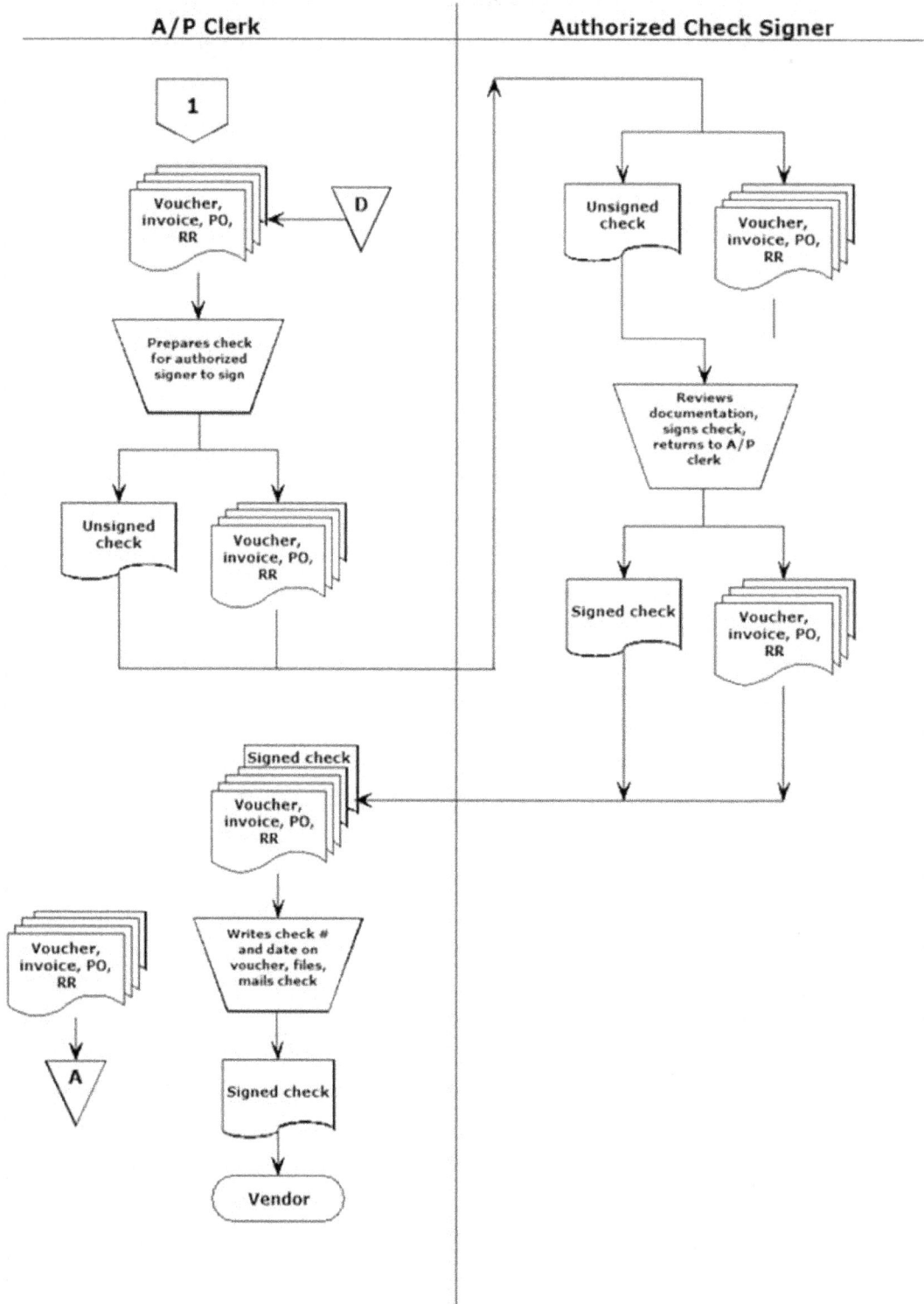

Exhibit 3.7 – Suggested document flowchart for Mokpo Ceramics A/P and cash disbursements activities (continued)

How did your document flowchart compare to the suggested drawing? Are there any aspects that confuse you? You are introduced to two new symbols in documenting the Mokpo Ceramics activities. Of course, you did not know these ahead of time and probably used your own icons to represent the concepts. The two new symbols are the storage (hard copy) location and the off-page connector.

The **storage symbol** is an upside down triangle or pyramid. It shows temporary or permanent storage for paper documents. In the Mokpo Ceramics document flowchart, we see it serving both purposes. On page 3-13, the purchase order and receiving report are retrieved from the temporary file called the *pending file*. It's where we keep documents that ultimately become part of the voucher package until the invoice is received and the voucher/voucher package is prepared. On page 3-14, the clerk writes the check number and payment date on the voucher and permanently files it in the vendor file.

The **off-page connector symbol** is valuable when the document flowchart extends across several pages. It is placed at the bottom of the column and sequentially numbered to show movement from one page to another.

In Summary

Documenting business processes and activities is an essential part of working with accounting information systems. Regardless of your role as a user, designer, or auditor of these systems, at some time you will need to learn about a task or activity. Perhaps you'll have to communicate with others about how something works. Flowcharts assist those who evaluate internal controls, helping them spot potential weaknesses or vulnerabilities.

In practice, accountants and auditors employ a variety of documentation tools and styles. While you've learned about two of them – the physical data flow diagram and document flowchart – a number of other graphical tools exist to explain activities and relationships including process flowcharts, systems flowcharts, and organization charts.

Once you've become familiar with the fundamentals of flowcharting (by means of physical data flow diagrams and document flowcharts), you can leverage those skills to efficiently learn how to work with other types of flowcharts.

Your understanding of flowcharting will be useful in the remainder of this textbook. In Chapter 4, we take a look at the subject of business processes. These were mentioned frequently in this chapter and like flowcharts, will feature prominently in Chapters 5 through 10.

Chapter Core Vocabulary

Computerized process symbol – shows an action performed by application software.

Connector symbol – directs the reader of a document flowchart to a discontiguous column on the flowchart.

Database storage symbol – identifies data retrieved from or stored in a database.

Decision symbol – identifies a closed-ended question (one answerable by a "yes" or "no") in a process or activity.

Display screen symbol – indicates a peripheral electronic device through which input or output is viewed.

Document flowchart – communicates the functional departments, people, or entities involved in the business activity or process and the documents used or created by them.

Document symbol – identifies paper documents that are used or created during a process or activity.

Keyboard/scan data entry symbol – depicts actions where data is entered into peripheral devices connected to computers.

Manual process symbol – documents a person's manual effort in a process or activity.

Off-page connector symbol – denotes movement from one page of a document flowchart to the next.

Physical data flow diagram – shows data sources (input), actions performed on the data (processing), and the processed data (output). It describes *how* data moves through a business process or activity (one segment of a process) and the *entities* (departments, offices, or people) involved in creating, updating, and using this data.

Requisitioner – an employee making a request to purchase a product or service from a supplier (vendor).

Storage symbol – shows data retrieved from or stored in a non-computerized storage location.

Terminator symbol–shows the beginning and ending points of the document flowchart. A document flowchart always begins and ends with a terminator symbol.

Chapter 4

Business processes

Chapter Core Questions

1. What is done in the finance business process?

2. What takes place in the human resources business process?

3. What is accomplished in the marketing business process?

4. What are some of the activities and tasks in the production and manufacturing/operations business process?

5. What is done in the product and business development business process?

6. What takes place in the supply chain business process?

7. What is accomplished in the sales business process?

8. What business processes are associated with not-for-profit organizations?

Introduction

Natureza.com was an early mover in online retailing for natural health and beauty products from around the globe. Its daily business activities require a smooth flow of data to support coordinated tasks that stretch across international boundaries. From its original business strategy developed in 2001 – selling cosmetics – to its newest marketplace initiatives, Natureza relies on a complex orchestration of people and information technologies.

In this chapter, we'll examine a collection of Natureza's business processes to form an understanding of the general business processes common to most organizations. Depicted here are examples of how such processes are structured. You must keep in mind that all entities run their business activities differently, so it's not possible to present a single model of how sales and customer service, manufacturing and logistics, investing, or human resources recruiting activities are structured.

And to add to your feeling of disorientation, no definitive collection of named business processes exists either. We will describe **business processes** as coordinated sets of complex tasks and practices that accomplish daily business activities. Unlike financial accounting where there are rather clear labels for financial statement elements (such as assets, liabilities, equity, revenues, expenses, gains, and losses), the categorization for business processes is less well defined. In this chapter we employ the business applications classifications noted by information technology company SAP[14].

Finance	Product/Business Development
Human Resources	Supply Chain
Marketing	Sales
Production/Manufacturing/Operations	

While not a universal set of classifications, they generally represent the major business processes found in most organizations. We shall employ these categories to envision the kinds of routine tasks and activities that occur at Natureza.com. In recognition of the unique dimensions of not-for-profit organizations, the chapter concludes with descriptions of several processes particular to them.

Chapter Core Question 1: What is done in the finance business process?

Finance

Encompassing a broad array of related activities, the **finance business process** would include Natureza.com's accounting, external reporting, budgeting, treasury, and debt/equity funding sub-processes.

> **Finance**
> Accounting
> External reporting
> Budgeting
> Treasury
> Debt/equity funding

Accounting

Journal entries. Adjustments. Financial statement preparation. Closing. A streamlined monthly accounting cycle is essential if Natureza wishes to collect, process, and communicate its accounting data to internal users. Receivables and payables are updated as daily sales and purchasing transactions occur. Cash receipts from customers and disbursements to vendors and employees are recorded. Employee travel expenses or product pricing plans might be examined and new practices developed in response to such analyses.

External reporting

As a publicly traded company, Natureza.com must comply with a number of external financial reporting regulations from the Securities and Exchange Commission. Ensuring accurate and timely preparation of financial data for the SEC, creditors, and investors is the domain of the external reporting subprocess. In collaboration with external accounting and tax experts, Natureza staffers involved in these activities strive for forthright and on-time production of required data.

Budgeting

From predicting next quarter's revenues for the Men's Skin Care line of products to forecasting next year's warehousing and utility expenses, Natureza's budgeting subprocess demands precision in response to the dynamic and sensitive retail sector in which it operates. Combining historical data from its accounting system with current sales and marketing estimates, Natureza's budget analysts develop and continuously refine the company's

---

14   SAP Solutions webpage, 2013. Available at: http://www.sap.com/solutions/index.epx

revenue, expense, and capital acquisition budgets. Depending on their needs, staffers demand flexibility in analyzing the budget data. Natureza's managers apply multidimensional analysis to various layers of data, and then recombine it in ways useful for their business decisions. Capital budgeting projects are conducted in collaboration with Natureza's debt and equity funding subprocesses.

Treasury

Cash management functions are central to an organization's desire to maintain liquidity without parking large amounts of cash in bank accounts. Natureza's treasury staff uses historical, current, and predicted cash flow data from the accounting information system and develops projections for the amounts and timing of short-term cash inflows and outflows. If these forecasts indicate a cash flow gap, Natureza's financial managers can decide from which sources it will raise the additional cash: issuing commercial paper, drawing down cash reserves, or liquidating marketable securities. The treasury subprocess also focuses on targets for longer-term investing: choosing from among suitable equity or debt instruments based on time and risk.

Debt and equity funding

How can Natureza raise large amounts of capital to finance major business initiatives? If it wanted to acquire another entity, would it do so by paying cash, borrowing, issuing bonds, or selling stock? Questions like these are typically decided by staffers working in the debt and equity funding subprocess. Natureza's finance professionals, in consultation with outside investment experts, would determine whether a bond issue or sale of additional company stock might be the most effective option for raising capital.

Chapter Core Question 2: What takes place in the human resources business process?

Human Resources

What does a typical day look like for those employed in the **human resources business process**? Like many large corporations, Natureza's human resources business process takes the lead in recruiting, assessing, hiring, and developing its staff. Further, several administrative and regulatory activities are carried out in the human resources business process: benefits administration and government reporting.

> **Human Resources**
> Recruiting
> Assessing/hiring
> Staff development
> Benefits administration
> Government reporting

Recruiting

How do you identify energetic, talented people to join and grow with your organization? It's a significant question, the work for which is charged to those involved in the recruiting subprocess. Natureza's Careers website is the portal through which the company searches for potential new staff. Other job-search sites, such as Monster.com and Natureza's links on LinkedIn and Facebook, publicize Natureza's job vacancies. The recruiting subprocess should inform prospective staffers about the company, its values, and the specific education and experience criteria for various jobs.

Assessing and hiring

After the company has collected applications from a pool of potential job candidates, Natureza's assessing and hiring subprocesses continue the work. Central to the activities are evaluating applicant quality and searching for those applicants whose profiles appear to fit with what Natureza is looking for. Once the candidate pool is narrowed down to a group of finalists, background checks and tests or interviews would be conducted. These typically would involve meetings with managers and staff in the department for which Natureza is hiring, as well as interactions with people from human resources.

After an offer is made to and accepted by the candidate, hiring activities would include enrolling the new hire in benefits programs, establishing an employee record in the HR information system, issuing identification and security credentials, and orienting the new hire. Some of these tasks would be performed at the local office in which the staffer works; other tasks might be delegated to the corporate human resources center and information technology department.

Staff development

What comes next in the lifecycle of employees? Natureza develops and grooms its staffers for their current and future work assignments. In-house education and training programs build staff skills and prepare people for their next roles. Career path planning and mentoring for mid-level managers might be offered. Relying on comprehensive profiles of its staffers, Natureza would form work teams for temporary or long-term projects. Learning takes place daily; staffers' experiences are managed and documented in ways that promote knowledge diffusion throughout the company.

Benefits administration

Another set of activities undertaken in the human resources business process likely appears invisible to most staffers. Teams of people are responsible for choosing and managing health and disability insurance, dependent care reimbursement plans, wellness initiatives, retirement programs, relocation assistance, and other benefits designed to attract and retain employees. In addition, people working in this subprocess assist employees and retirees with their questions and problems about the benefit programs.

Government reporting

Every organization is required to communicate certain demographic and event data to government entities. Whether work-related injuries or illnesses for the Occupational Safety & Health Administration, or compensation and unemployment data for the Bureau of Labor Statistics, entities must record, organize, and make periodic reports to varied municipal, state, and federal government agencies. The human resources information system needs to accumulate data in a manner compliant with government reporting requirements.

Chapter Core Question 3: What is accomplished in the marketing business process?

Marketing

The **marketing business process** complements the sales business process, which we will review later in the chapter. Most organizations consider marketing as those sub-processes that identify what should be sold, to whom, and at what price/ combination with other items. Marketing also develops the strategies and tactics to carry out these activities. At Natureza.com, the first-mover and a leader in online marketing and sales, the marketing process might comprise product, service, and brand management, and customer relationship management.

> **Marketing**
> Product, service, and
> brand management
> Customer relationship
> management

Product, service, and brand management

Who would have thought the way goods are packaged for shipping could be studied, redesigned, and simplified for customers? Natureza did. Collaborating with vendors to produce more customer-friendly packaging for products sold by Natureza is a small example of product, service, and brand management.

Some of the more common activities in product, service, and brand management would include *selecting the products to offer* across the company's varied departments – including Men's Skin Care, Fragrances, Women's Cosmetics, and Bath & Hair Care, among others. As well, Natureza makes decisions about *how to create product combinations to increase sales.* Consider a shopper who wants to buy shampoo and conditioner. She's selected the orange blossom shampoo and green tea conditioner. Natureza further entices this customer by listing products frequently purchased by other customers who have bought the green tea conditioner. Product, service, and brand management is all about choosing the best products and services to offer for the brands carried by the merchandiser. And strategic thinking about consumer behavior is essential when developing the long-term trajectory of Natureza.com's own brand.

Customer relationship management

Creating a marketing experience tailored for each customer is the pinnacle of customer relationship management (CRM). To illustrate this marketing business subprocess, let's turn to an actual example using Amazon.com instead of a fictitious health and beauty products online retailer.

Amazon.com leverages its information technology innovations in a way that elevates CRM to an art form that has been imitated by many consumer retail websites. Consider how the company provides product and service recommendations to customers once they've logged in at Amazon's website.

As I was writing this book in Korea, it was my habit in the late afternoon to download the streaming audio of National Public Radio's afternoon news program *All Things Considered*. One day I listened to a news story about the upcoming Latin GRAMMY Awards. One of the artists featured in the story was celebrated Cuban singer Bebo Valdes. I immediately opened and pointed a Web browser to Amazon.com, then searched for the album mentioned on the radio program. I was interested in buying it, so added it to my Wish List, another Amazon.com CRM application. Days later, the next time I logged onto the site, Amazon incorporated that choice into its music recommendations for me.

Amazon's "Look Inside" feature offers previews of selected pages from books, and "Listen to Samples" provides 30-second music sound bites. Editor and customer reviews add a final touch to its on-site marketing efforts. While e-coupons and advertisements sent to customer social media sites might not be personalized, they are delivered in a convenient manner that encourages customers to click directly from advertisements and coupons to Amazon.com.

Chapter Core Question 4: What are some of the activities and tasks in the production and manufacturing/operations business processes?

Production and Manufacturing

The **production and manufacturing business process** consists of a cluster of activities allowing an entity to manage its raw materials and convert these raw materials into finished goods for sale to customers. Natureza.com is an online retailer and doesn't have production or manufacturing activities. But consider one of the company's suppliers, Catarina Cosmetics, and some of the typical tasks comprising its production and manufacturing business process.

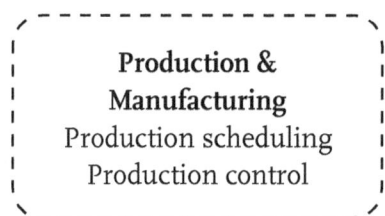

> **Production & Manufacturing**
> Production scheduling
> Production control

Production scheduling

How does Catarina Cosmetics know what, when, and how much to produce? Based on Catarina's sales projections (push manufacturing philosophy) or actual customer orders (pull philosophy), it schedules equipment, raw materials, parts, subassemblies, and staff in a fashion that facilitates the production of various cosmetics in time and on budget. Catarina, before it commits to making and delivering products to its retail customers, needs to review manufacturing schedules for all of the jobs it's obliged to complete. Tight coordination of factory fixed assets, people, and materials are required to meet customers' production specifications and delivery demands.

Production control

Once raw materials are brought to the manufacturing floor, staffers monitor the progress of various jobs in production. When troubles pop up, they are assessed and the daily manufacturing plan of action (schedule) is revised to reflect any production delays. This data is referenced by production staffers throughout the day to control hourly, daily, and weekly production schedules. As tasks are completed and work-in-process moves from stage to stage, the production control database is updated until the point where the finished goods are complete.

Operations

The **operations business process** will take on different names depending on the nature of the entity. As a merchandiser (retailer), Natureza.com doesn't make products for sale to retailers or consumers in the same way Catarina Cosmetics produces its eyeliner, foundation, or lipstick. Rather than refer to *manufacturing* at Natureza, we'll designate this business process *operations*. We shall consider the operations business process as those activities providing support to an organization's core sales and supply chain business processes.

> **Operations**
> Information technology
> Physical plant
> Public relations
> Customer service

Information technology

The survival of Natureza.com depends on a nearly zero-down-time information technology infrastructure. Customers around the globe expect to reach a fully functional retail website each time they log on. Natureza.com must maintain its hardware, networks, application and systems software, and keep its content current. These include information links with vendors, suppliers, customers, and other external stakeholders. And don't forget all of the company's applications in support of internal business processes such as finance and human resources. These too must be updated and perform on demand.

Physical plant services

Natureza's global corporate office is located in Horseheads, New York. In addition to its corporate facilities there, Natureza has physical facilities to conduct fulfillment, warehousing, and customer service activities. These are scattered across North America, Europe, and Asia. They must be cleaned, maintained, and periodically renovated or modified. Whether it's the customer service center in Constitution, Ohio, or regional business offices in Laramie, Wyoming, or Yinchuan, China, management and oversight of the physical plant is necessary. Safe, clean, and efficiently designed physical facilities promote creativity and collaboration across Natureza's core and supporting business processes.

Public relations

Entities must be able to clearly explain their vision, mission, goals, operating results, financial performance, and respond to events affecting them. Public relations activities encompass internal and external audiences, and determine what kind of information to share and how to communicate it with these constituents. Ranging from the Investor Relations Office's release of quarterly operating results to internal documents detailing announcements for new products or services, the public relations subprocess presents the private and public "face" of the entity.

Customer service

Supporting customers and handling their questions and problems – before and after the sale – constitutes a significant portion of the work of staffers in the customer service subprocess.

Chapter Core Question 5: What is done in the product and business development business process?

Product and Business Development

In how many new directions has Natureza.com grown since it first opened in January 2003? Expanding from its original product line of women's cosmetics, it jumped into women's and men's skin care, fragrances, and bath & hair care. It spread out internationally, to places such as Malaysia, Chile, and Portugal. And its scope of business operations extends beyond beauty and health retailer Natureza.com to include the Natureza Channel (available via satellite TV) and Health by Natureza magazine.

> **Product & Business Development**
> Strategy and planning
> Market opportunity scanning
> Collaboration and development
> Innovation management

Where did the seeds of these initiatives take root? In all likelihood, not in one specific department or place. Creativity and ingenuity cannot be harnessed into a single business process, but is fostered and nurtured throughout the entity. However, once new initiatives are adopted they tend to be assigned to a particular division or office to provide leadership and advocacy of the venture.

Here, our aim in discussing the **product and business development process** isn't to focus on the responsibilities of a fixed group of people housed inside a single business process. Instead, we'll attempt to depict three subprocesses that would take place across Natureza.com and its subsidiary entities. Product and business development doesn't necessarily happen in a neat and structured way in a single department; therefore, this portion of the chapter may seem similarly untidy!

Strategy and planning

Executives across Natureza's business entities continuously work on long range strategizing and planning. What should the company be doing three to 10 years from now? How can those strategies be turned into short-term and longer range action steps? Will entire divisions or business units be terminated or sold to other online retailers in the future? What does the future mix of products and services look like? Experience, perspectives, and information from across the company are distilled to create a long-term roadmap for Natureza.

Market opportunity scanning

At times, opportunities seem to present themselves with the least amount of warning. Let's return to an actual company, Amazon.com, and view this excerpt about competition from its 2008 annual report:

"Our businesses are rapidly evolving and intensely competitive. Our current and potential competitors include: (1) physical-world retailers, publishers, vendors, distributors, manufacturers and producers of our products; (2) other online e-commerce and mobile e-commerce sites, including sites that sell or distribute digital content; (3) a number of indirect competitors, including media companies, Web portals, comparison shopping websites, and Web search engines, either directly or in collaboration with other retailers; (4) companies that provide e-commerce services, including website development, fulfillment and customer service; (5) companies that provide infrastructure web services or other information storage or computing services or products; and (6) companies that design, manufacture, market or sell digital media devices.[15]

In any of these six areas of competition, Amazon might see a chance to take advantage of a change in the business environment and then make an acquisition to strengthen its competitive stance in a given market. Scanning

---

15   Amazon.com 2008 Form 10-K, page 4. Available at:
     http://phx.corporate-ir.net/External.File?item=UGFyZW50SUQ9MjAyN3xDaGlsZElEPS0xfFR5cGU9Mw==&t=1

the external environment for opportunities (as well as recognizing the related threats) permits companies to grow, expand, and take advantage of the early signs of market movements.

Collaboration and development / innovation management

Natureza.com collaborates with suppliers to create approximately 30 percent of its new products. Finding the right supplier partners with whom ideas and technology can be shared is a major endeavor characterized by complex interrelationships of ideas and people across the globe. Without innovation, Natureza.com, too, can fall victim to the pressures of competition. Its business partnerships with external entities help it innovate and enter new dimensions of retailing and complementary services.

Chapter Core Question 6: What takes place in the supply chain business process?

Supply Chain

Working with thousands of vendors and suppliers 24 hours a day, seven days a week, Natureza.com demands the highest level of accuracy and communication among members of its **supply chain**. Natureza's worldwide supply chain must function with near-zero faults; the subprocesses used to evaluate and choose suppliers, manage inventory levels, and ensure timely delivery and payment of purchases are tightly interwoven with sales and operations business processes.

Evaluating and choosing suppliers

Will Natureza.com do business with any supplier or vendor that asks? No. It will evaluate potential supply chain partners according to rigorous criteria. Only after Natureza identifies suppliers that are able to offer desired products at appropriate costs, can meet stringent fulfillment standards, and surpass expectations of quality and value will Natureza add those partners to its family of suppliers. Once part of Natureza's supply chain, these vendors must deliver ongoing quality and value to Natureza and its customers. Throughout the chain, suppliers' products and services are continuously assessed to determine Natureza's product mix and respond to its customers' demands.

Managing inventory levels; ensuring timely delivery and payment of purchases

Few things are worse for retailers – both online and physical – than having to tell customers that the items they want to buy are out of stock. Natureza.com relies on historical sales data and sales forecasts to identify appropriate stock levels, automatic reorder points, and optimal inventory order quantities. Purchase orders, shipping notices, transportation inquiries, and receiving reports are electronically communicated between Natureza.com and its supply chain partners. Solid forecasting and on-time delivery of purchases by suppliers and transportation companies helps Natureza minimize inventory stock-outs, keeping customers and supply chain partners satisfied. It's also important to keep suppliers and vendors satisfied – meaning to pay promptly for purchases. Accounts payable and cash disbursement activities are linked to the supply chain and connect the supply chain business process to the finance business process.

Chapter Core Question 7: What is accomplished in the sales business process?

Sales

Like many physical and online retailers, two of Natureza.com's single largest sales days are Black Friday and Cyber Monday. From receiving customer orders to shipping the goods and communicating order status with customers, Natureza depends on tight coordination of different departments and locations to carry out its successful and efficient sales activities. So what's involved in the **sales business process**? Of course, the starting point is the receipt of a

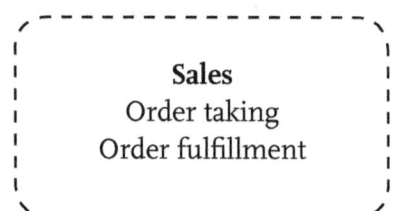

Sales
Order taking
Order fulfillment

sales order from the customer. Following receipt of the order, the company fulfills and ships the products. It is critical for Natureza.com to maintain frequent and accurate communication with its customers throughout all steps in the sales business process.

Order taking

What are you buying today? Is it lip balm, men's body wash, or the orange and guarana-infused shampoo and conditioner? It all starts at the Natureza.com retail Web site. Customers log in then add products to their shopping cart. When customers finish shopping, they move to the checkout phase of the transaction. Here, they choose the delivery address and method, and indicate form of payment (credit or debit card, gift card, discounts, coupons, etc.). Based on these circumstances, Natureza calculates the total sales price (which may include state and municipal sales taxes according to state law and degree of business presence in the state). Customers get one last chance to review order details before processing. During processing, Natureza validates the form of payment and delivery address. Exceptions, such as incorrect, expired or rejected credit card numbers, or delivery addresses that don't match those on file with the U.S. Postal Service, are communicated to customers for correction.

Order fulfillment

After processing the sale order, Natureza needs to determine from which distribution center(s) the order will be filled. It's possible that the lip balm and men's body wash will be shipped from its Cheyenne, Wyoming, fulfillment center, while the shampoo and conditioner come from Cross Lanes, West Virginia. Staffers at fulfillment centers receive sales orders, pick goods from storage locations, pack products into boxes, review orders for completeness and correctness, and arrange shipping according to customer delivery instructions. Once orders are shipped, Natureza notifies customers. Items on backorder or other reasons for delivery delays also would be communicated to customers.

This introduction to business processes – using Natureza.com as an illustrative entity – provides you with a foundational overview of the significant tasks and activities common to many medium- and large-sized entities. Remember, the specific tasks, scale, complexity of business processes and subprocesses vary according to the size and nature of the entity. But in general, this chapter introduces you to the departments, staffers, routines, and practices you will encounter in the remaining chapters of this textbook.

Before we conclude the chapter, it's important to include a short discussion of some of the business processes unique to and at the core of not-for-profit organizations. Certainly, Natureza.com will not serve as a relevant example for this conversation. Instead, we'll use an organization called the Osborne Senior Center.

Chapter Core Question 8: What business processes are associated with not-for-profit organizations?

Processes Significant to Not-for-Profit Organizations

Consider Nationwide Children's Hospital, Friends of Strays, Habitat for Humanity, First United Methodist Church, the Pinellas County Science Center, and the Memphis Botanic Garden. What do they have in common? Yes, all of them are not-for-profit organizations (NFPOs). Not-for-profit organizations carry out a diverse collection of pursuits in social, civic, educational, cultural, medical, and religious settings. The primary characteristic of NFPOs is their absence of a profit motive and a compulsion to return earnings to the owners. The International Center for Not-for-Profit Law explains this:

"It is possible that such an organization will in fact make a profit from time to time, but that is not the principal purpose for which it is organized and operated. Nor is its purpose to distribute any portion of any profit for private gain. The

major distinguishing characteristic between not-for-profit and for-profit organizations is that the former are governed by the principle of non-distribution." [16]

A caution flag: don't be misled into thinking that not-for-profit organizations lack marketing, human resources, finance, operations, supply chain, and program development processes. Similar to for-profit entities, NFPOs must raise capital, purchase goods and services, promote their services, collect service fees, hire and cultivate staff, and pay bills. Your understanding of for-profit business processes easily can be transferred to the NFPO environment, allowing you to compare and contrast characteristics of both.

This section of the chapter addresses three business processes of particular significance to not-for-profit organizations: stakeholder stewardship, program cost accounting, and annual reporting to the Internal Revenue Service (IRS). Most NFPOs acquire their operating and capital resources from individuals, foundations, and various government units. Whether the resources are cash, tangible assets, or gifts of investment instruments, NFPOs are obligated to be responsible stewards of these assets and accurately account for their use. As well as providing accounting data for external stakeholders, NFPOs have internal stakeholders (staff, executives, trustees or directors) whose accounting information needs must be met. Finally, NFPOs that meet certain minimum gross receipts levels must file an annual information return to the IRS, the Form 990. We'll illustrate the stakeholder stewardship, program cost accounting, and Form 990 reporting processes by examining the Osborne Senior Center, a non-residential daytime center offering social activities, meals, and support to senior citizens in Osborne County, Nebraska.

STOP. Find a classmate and make a list of people and entities you imagine might provide funds to the Osborne Center. Think as broadly as possible. After you've made your list, read on.

Stakeholder stewardship

Does your list of donors and funding sources include individuals and entities such as the following?

Local/county government	Local/regional businesses
State government	Religious organizations
Federal government	Service foundations (*e.g.* United Way)
Local or regional agencies on aging	Private (individual) foundations
Community citizens	Corporate foundations

The Osborne Senior Center might receive donations from people living in the county and surrounding regions, local/regional businesses, religious organizations, and local chapters of service organizations such as the Red Cross, United Way, Rotary, or Lions. Local government units might contribute a small portion of their tax revenues to the Osborne Center. In essence, the government is outsourcing certain types of senior citizen services (hot lunches for the elderly living on fixed incomes, routine medical screenings, transportation, or eldercare), shifting the work and related costs to the private sector. Thus, it's not inappropriate for the government to share a small portion of its tax or fee revenues with the Center.

State and federal government agencies might offer grants to NFPOs that provide certain programs and services for the elderly. If the Osborne Center wanted to become a site for the Foster Grandparent Program (FGP), it might write a grant application to the Corporation for National and Community Service, or request funds from

16   Frequently Asked Questions, The International Center for Not-for-Profit Law, 2012. Available at: http://www.icnl.org/contact/faq/index.html

a regional agency on aging that already received an FGP grant from the federal government. Service organizations, individuals, or corporate foundations might make donations to NFPOs or invite applications for grants on a variety of programmatic themes.

 Regardless of the source of the resources, the Osborne Senior Center needs to carefully record the amounts and types of assets received and the use to which they were put. In the case of donations made by individuals, businesses, or foundations, the Osborne Center is required to prepare an annual acknowledgment of gifts received. This is a good business practice as well as a requirement of the Internal Revenue Service. State laws typically prescribe the format and content for quarterly and annual reports delivered to municipal and state governments. Foundation or government grant-making agencies generally require an accounting of how grant resources were used and may dictate the manner in which the information is communicated.

Program cost accounting

In addition to tracking program expenses for its stakeholders, not-for-profit organizations like the Osborne Senior Center have managerial (internal) accounting information needs. Budgets must be created, current expenses and revenues recorded, and end-of-period budget variances determined and investigated. The Center's management and staff rely on this data to operate within the limits of its resources. When new activities are being considered, managers can refer to similar programs' costs, extract relevant data, and use it to forecast costs for these new activities. Management and Osborne Center trustees also would refer to the data in deciding whether certain programs and services can continue to be offered.

And should the Osborne Center ever face a situation where programmatic cuts are needed, data from the program cost accounting system can be extracted and what-if analyses performed to determine how best to undertake program cost reductions without sacrificing service quality.

Internal Revenue Service reporting

Not-for-profit organizations and charities with gross receipts in excess of $200,000 will file the Internal Revenue Service's (IRS) annual information return, Form 990[17], *Return of Organization Exempt from Income Tax*[18]. NFPOs must file various supplemental schedules if, for instance, they are involved with political campaign and lobbying activities, conduct educational activities, have international activities, issue bonds, or conduct transactions with related parties.

With the broadened disclosure requirements, not-for-profit organizations like the Osborne Center must have information systems that can easily provide the needed data in a convenient reporting format. NFPOs that cannot extract details for their Form 990 or Form 990-EZ filings will have a time-consuming task of manually mining their files and documents to obtain the data. Even the most information technology-savvy NFPOs likely will need to comb through various evidential sources to secure some of the non-financial data asked for in the Form 990 and its accompanying schedules.

The Osborne Senior Center should preview IRS information requirements and create mechanisms to capture, process, and store data in support of the annual information reporting process.

In Summary

Understanding the basic business processes is necessary to create and maintain an effective and efficient accounting information system. Additionally, the work of auditors is streamlined when the AIS they're auditing is well

17   Internal Revenue Service, Form 990, 2012. Available at: http://www.irs.gov/pub/irs-pdf/f990.pdf

18   Most organizations with gross receipts of $200,000 or less can use the Form 990-EZ. Available at: http://www.irs.gov/pub/irs-pdf/f990ez.pdf

designed and documented. Stretching across the entity's range of activities, integrated collections of tasks and jobs enable an entity to serve customers and work with vendors.

Using Natureza.com and the Osborne Senior Center, two fictitious organizations, we examined the more common business processes. Finance encompasses the accounting, external reporting, budgeting, treasury, and debt/equity funding sub-processes. Human resources handles recruiting, assessing, hiring, and developing staff. Managing products, services, and brands and customer relationships comprise the world of marketing. Producing its products and supporting the entity's core revenue-generating activities are under the scope of the operations and manufacturing business processes.

Product and business development might consist of strategy and planning, market opportunity scanning, and innovation management. The supply chain process evaluates and chooses suppliers, manages inventory levels, and ensures timely delivery of purchases. The sales business process involves taking and filling customer orders.

In addition to the seven processes described, not-for-profit organizations have several business processes particular to their needs, including donor management and accountability, program accounting, and tax reporting.

Why should you be concerned about having a solid grounding in the business processes? The remainder of the textbook examines each of the business processes, paying close attention to the internal controls that can strengthen the processes. In Chapter 5, we examine the sales business process.

Chapter Core Vocabulary

Business processes – coordinated sets of complex tasks and practices that accomplish daily business activities.

Finance business process – encompasses accounting, external reporting, budgeting, treasury, and debt/equity funding activities.

Human resources business process – includes recruiting, assessing, hiring, and developing staff, as well as handling benefits administration and government reporting.

Marketing business process – activities that identify what should be sold, to whom, and at what price/combination with other items. It develops the strategies and tactics to carry out these activities.

Operations business process–those activities providing support to an organization's core sales and supply chain business processes.

Product and business development process – the institution-wide collection of activities that foster the creation of new products and services.

Production and manufacturing business process – a cluster of activities allowing an entity to manage its raw materials and convert these raw materials into finished goods for sale to customers.

Sales business process – the activities to evaluate customer credit, receive and fulfill customer orders, service customers after the sale, and manage customer relations.

Supply chain business process – the collection of activities to evaluate and choose suppliers, manage inventory levels, and ensure timely and accurate delivery of inventory from suppliers.

Chapter 5

Sales business process: sales and order fulfillment; accounts receivable

Chapter Core Questions

1. What are the typical data flows and internal control hot spots in the sales and order fulfillment subprocess?

2. How does data flow through the accounts receivable and cash receipts subprocess and what are the internal control vulnerabilities in this subprocess?

Introduction

Among the largest pharmaceutical companies in the world. A company history of close to 90 years. Headquartered in Oxford, Mississippi. Sales in more than 75 countries. Employs nearly 81,000 people across the globe. Has launched drug products for diabetes, depression, cancer, and cardiac disease. Which company is it?

Bardia Pharmaceutical. Bardia sells its products directly to large retailers and drug wholesalers in the United States and abroad. We will examine how data flows through the sales business process using representative transactions of the fictitious global corporation Bardia Pharmaceutical. The chapter relies on data flow diagrams to help you learn about these data flows and highlight internal controls that might help Bardia deter, detect, and limit weaknesses in its **sales business process**, the collection of subprocesses related to the revenue earning process. These encompass sales and order fulfillment, and accounts receivable and cash receipts.

This chapter requires you to apply knowledge from Chapter 2 (the ASSRAV internal control toolkit) and Chapter 3 (basic flowcharting) so you can understand the data flows, identify vulnerabilities in the sales business process, and design effective internal controls for the process.

Before we move into the first chapter core question, it will be helpful to review the definition of revenues.

"Revenues are inflows or other enhancements of assets of an entity or settlements of its liabilities (or a combination of both) from delivering or producing goods, rendering services, or other activities that constitute the entity's ongoing major or central operations."[19]

---

19   Statement of Financial Accounting Concepts No. 6, *Elements of Financial Statements*. Paragraph 78. Financial Accounting Standards Board. Norwalk, CT. December 1985. Available at: http://www.fasb.org/pdf/aop_CON6.pdf

You were first exposed to this definition in your accounting principles course and would have delved more deeply into the topic of revenues in intermediate accounting. However, in the accounting information systems course you won't be making journal entries or adjusting entries involving revenue recognition. Instead, the emphasis is on understanding the flow of accounting data through the sales business process – from sale order to cash receipts. Let's get to it!

Chapter Core Question 1: What are the typical data flows and internal control hot spots in the sales and order fulfillment subprocess?

Data Flows/Internal Controls in the Sales and Order Fulfillment Subprocess

To whom does a pharmaceutical company sell its products? Jot down a short list of customers. Would it include the final consumers, people like you and me, who take the drugs for hypertension, infections, or diabetes? No. Pharmaceutical companies typically sell to wholesalers, who in turn sell to hospitals, doctors' offices (health care providers), and retail pharmacies. And some sell directly to the entities identified in the previous sentence. Consider the following scenario to illustrate our discussion about sales.

Suppose Bardia sells its drug Melbase – used to treat the symptoms of altitude sickness – to Fernie Biopharma, a pharmaceutical distribution and services company. What would be the sequence of activities you'd expect to see in this business-to-business sale transaction? STOP. Find a partner and write down the steps involved. Until you're finished, please don't read further!

Here's a general description of the likely steps.

1. Fernie Biopharma (customer) prepares purchase order and transmits to Bardia.

2. After Bardia receives Fernie's purchase order, enters data into sales module (likely using an ERP system) and creates sales order.

3. Inventory stocks checked to determine if order can be fulfilled in its entirety.

4. Out-of-stock items tagged for backorder status.

5. Based on amounts that can be shipped to Fernie and according to delivery instructions, delivery costs added and final sales order amount calculated.

6. Sales order amount compared to Fernie's available credit to see if order can be processed on account.

7. If sales order total is less than available credit balance, sales invoice generated. If not, credit department contacted and accounts receivable balance/credit issues resolved. Sales invoice generated.

8. Bardia's fulfillment center picks and boxes products, prepares packing slip, and ships order to Fernie.

9. Bardia transmits sales invoice to Fernie.

Take note: throughout the steps in the sales and order fulfillment subprocess, Bardia would send status reports to Fernie Biopharma to communicate progress on the order. Think about what transpires when you order something from Amazon.com. You receive a confirmation of your order and a notice when the goods are shipped. Business-to-business sales transactions use similar communication techniques to keep all parties informed about the order's status.

Now let's use those flowcharting skills from Chapter 3 to draw a physical data flow diagram (DFD) of this subprocess. It will help you visualize from where data comes, what is done with it, and to where the processed data moves. Later on, we'll use this DFD to help identify internal control hot spots (vulnerabilities) and suggest control activities using Chapter 2's ASSRAV toolkit.

Exhibit 5.1 – Bardia Pharmaceutical DFD for Sales and Order Fulfillment Subprocess

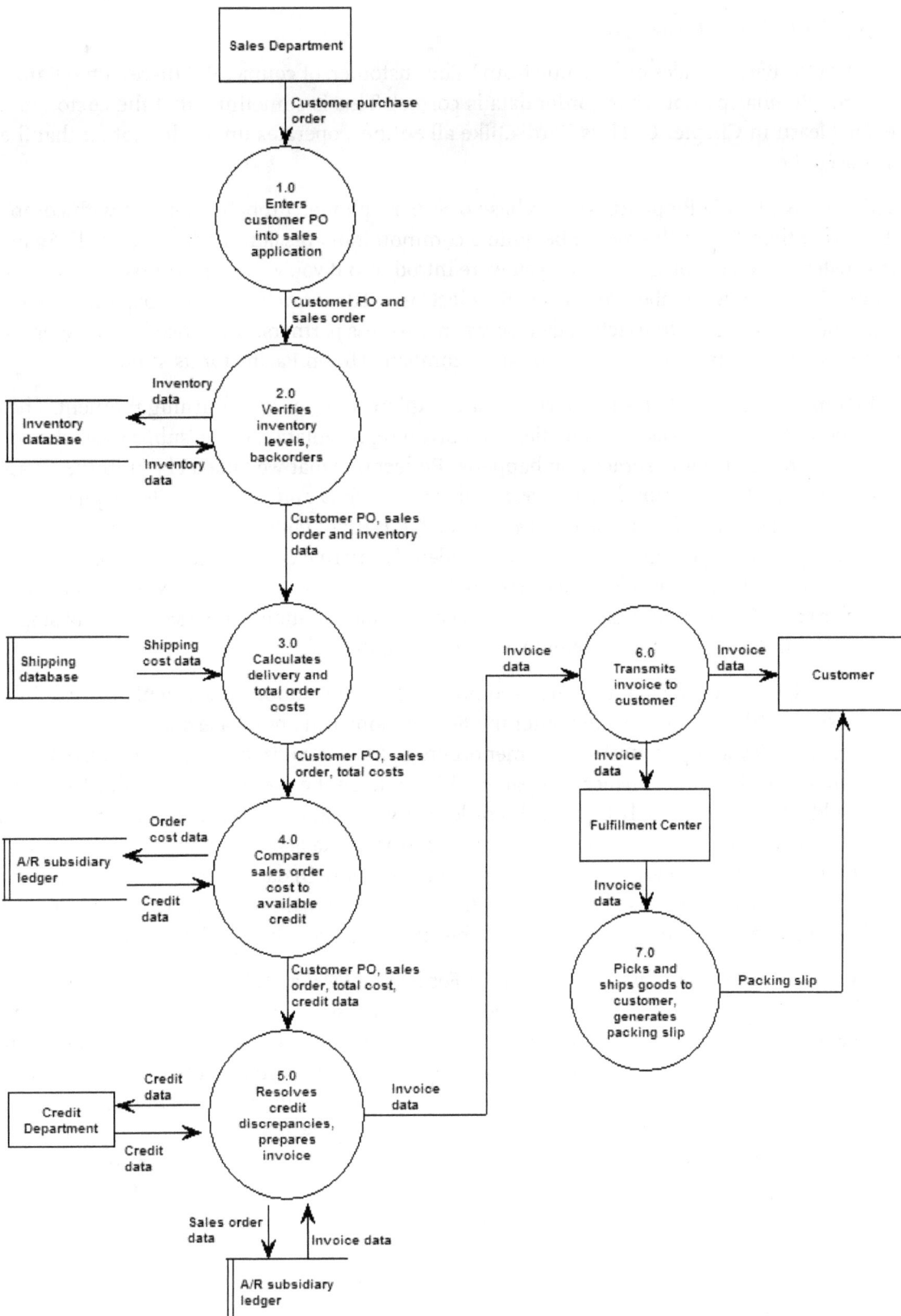

Does your data flow diagram resemble the one shown in Exhibit 5.1? Good. Now you're ready to consider the sources of, processes performed on, and destinations for the data in the sales subprocess.

Sales and order fulfillment subprocess data flows

Where does the data for Bardia's sales order come from? The customer, of course. But there's little Bardia can do to ensure Fernie Biopharma's purchase order data is correct. This is something that the customer must assure, as we shall learn in Chapter 6. Thus Bardia, like all entities, operates under the notion that the customer's order is accurate.

How does Bardia receive Fernie Biopharma's purchase order? By phone? Probably not, but with companies that are much smaller than Bardia this would be quite a common transmission mode. By e-mail? Again, not likely, but think instead of a technology to which you were introduced if you've taken a course in management information systems. Do you remember? Yes, it's EDI – **electronic data interchange** – the paperless, electronic means of communicating standard transaction data between business partners. If you need a refresher on EDI, take a look at the information provided by transportation company Union Pacific for its suppliers[20].

Talking about EDI makes me want to take a short detour to explore an important learning moment. The flowcharts in this textbook depict the tasks and activities for a broad representation of the subprocess; they do not convey the single and definitive way something happens. Reflect on what we talked about in the Chapter 4 introduction: *Remember, all entities run their business activities differently and it's not possible to present a single model of how customer service, cash disbursements, investing, or HR benefits administration activities are conducted.* So as we describe business activities, draw flowcharts, and identify internal control weaknesses from this point forward, please consider that they represent a basic view of business transactions and activities. It's not feasible to include a flowchart or internal control assessment for each possible variation of how sales, purchasing, fixed assets, operations, and human resources are conducted in every entity.

Okay, let's return to the series of steps in the sales and order fulfillment subprocess articulated in Exhibit 5.1. Think about process 1.0. Who at Bardia would enter the Fernie Biopharma purchase order data into the sales application? Is there a clerk waiting to receive customer orders and key them into the sales module? I wouldn't expect it happening at Bardia, but at smaller companies this could be the method employed. At Bardia, EDI transmissions would be received directly by the sales order software, processed, and a sales order generated. The power of EDI rests in the ability to import, process, and export data across various applications without having to enter it multiple times. Provided the original purchase order (PO) data is correct, Bardia's sales order, shipping charges, and invoice should also be accurate. [But what about smaller companies that don't use EDI? A clerk manually enters data into the sales system from the customer's purchase order.]

Once this task is completed, Bardia's output consists of the Fernie Biopharma PO data and the Bardia sales order data. Can the sales order be processed at this point? No, it's first necessary to check the on-hand quantities of items ordered by Fernie Biopharma. It is bad business practice to bill the customer for goods that are currently unavailable. Units reported on the sales invoice, which will be generated later in the subprocess, should be tied to the quantity of products delivered to the customer. Process 2.0 in Exhibit 5.1 reflects this facet of the sales and order fulfillment subprocess. To what would we refer in checking real-time inventory status? Bardia's sales software should incorporate this step immediately upon entry of the SKU or UPC bar code data, comparing the units entered with on-hand quantities reported from the inventory database. Out-of-stock and backordered items would be flagged and the sales order adjusted to reflect on-hand quantities.

---

20   Union Pacific Suppliers EDI webpage, 2013. Available at: http://www.uprr.com/suppliers/account/stedmf/index.shtml

How might this be accomplished by a smaller company? In fact, with barcoding technology and daily system updates it's not too difficult for smaller companies to keep perpetual inventory records. But even if these tools are beyond the means of some small entities, weekly counts or visual inspections of products on hand can be used to approximate inventory levels. Little could be worse than failing to give a customer timely communication about product unavailability. A customer does not want to receive an order confirmation today only to be told tomorrow or the following day that one or more of the items ordered is out of stock.

Process 3.0 in Exhibit 5.1 explains that Bardia calculates the freight costs to ship the order to the customer. How does the company accurately make these calculations? Relying on a database of shipping charges based on product weight, distance, and customer shipping preference, Bardia can determine shipping costs and add those to the total sales order amount. What if this information was not stored in a database? How might smaller companies ascertain shipping charges to be billed to their customers? Weights need to be calculated for all products sold. Total weight can be measured by multiplying unit weights and the quantities to be shipped. With a total weight, tables provided by transportation companies (typically available online) can be consulted for the total freight cost. If not accessible online, phone calls would be made to the transportation companies' customer service centers.

Once total invoice costs are computed, process 4.0 in Exhibit 5.1 compares it to the customer's available line of credit. Companies determine accounts receivable credit limits for each customer based on such factors as credit history, size, type of customer, and credit risk. Prior to final authorization of the sale, Bardia consults its accounts receivable subsidiary ledger to determine if Fernie Biopharma's outstanding accounts receivable balance – plus the amount of the pending sale – would keep the firm within its credit limit.

Refer to process 5.0. Bardia processes the sale transaction as long as the new balance is under Fernie Biopharma's credit limit. But if the amount of the pending sale pushes the customer's outstanding receivables balance over its credit limit, what would Bardia do? Reject the sale? Not likely, particularly if the customer is a strong, long-time customer. But who at Bardia would grant the approval to raise a customer's credit limit or grant an exception for the pending sale?

Generally, the credit manager or another member of the accounting or finance staff would be entrusted with this authority. But why not allow the sales department representative or a sales manager make the decision? Let's hold off answering that question until we discuss sales and order fulfillment internal control weaknesses.

Now that the invoice has been prepared, process 6.0 shows it being transmitted to Fernie Biopharma. How does this happen? If you guessed that Bardia might use EDI, you're probably correct. Alternately, companies might generate hard copy invoices and mail or fax them to their customers.

At last, staffers in Bardia's fulfillment center would pick products from the shelves based on the data from the invoice, package those goods, and prepare a packing slip evidencing the contents of the box. Process 7.0 shows these tasks. Finally, the box containing the goods and the packing slip would be shipped to the customer. In the case of a large company such as Bardia, electronic communication of the packing slip data, shipping date, and expected delivery date would be sent to Fernie Biopharma.

Sales and order fulfillment subprocess internal controls

Now that you have a fundamental knowledge of the steps in the sales sub-process, it's time to turn attention to the matter of internal controls. Once more, please examine the physical data flow diagram in Exhibit 5.1. Recall from Chapter 2 that the purpose of incorporating internal controls into our daily business tasks is to deter, detect, and reduce the impact of business risks and threats. Try to identify potential hot spots (weaknesses, vulnerabilities) in the activities of this subprocess. Are there places where authorization, supervision, segregation of duties, records and documentation, access to assets, or verification (ASSRAV) should be taking place but aren't?

STOP. Following the format and example shown below, create a list of the potential vulnerabilities for each step in the sales and order fulfillment subprocess. To the right of each item in your list, identify one or more internal controls you'd adopt to lessen the effect of these weaknesses. Also note which of the six ASSRAV tools is associated with your internal control suggestion. Don't read on until you've finished your list.

Potential Vulnerabilities (Process No.)	Suggested Internal Control	ASSRAV Tool
Clerk enters incorrect data into sales order software (Process 1.0)	Sales order software performs edit tests (validity, reasonableness, completeness) on data entered into sales order	Verification

With your list completed, let's review these weaknesses and vulnerabilities of the sales and order fulfillment subprocess.

Potential Vulnerabilities (Process No.)	Suggested Internal Control	ASSRAV Tool
Inventory database reflects incorrect inventory quantities due to shrinkage (2.0)	Occasional audits of database records against actual inventory quantities; security cameras monitor activity in inventory warehouse	Verification Supervision
Shipping database contains out-of-date costs, leading to incorrect cost calculations (3.0)	Ensure most current cost data is pulled from transportation companies' databases	Records and documentation
Sales clerk adjusts sales prices or gives discounts (3.0)	Supervisor or manager approval needed for sales price adjustments	Authorization
A/R subsidiary ledger data inaccurate (4.0)	Periodic reconciliations of ledger balances with customers' records of amounts owed	Verification
Customer account problems handled by sales clerk instead of credit department (5.0)	Sales order software prohibits sales clerk from adjusting account balances (read-only access) and allows only credit department adjustments	Authorization, separation of duties
Credit department issues customer credit or writes off account balances in excess of amount deemed appropriate (5.0)	Credit department manager reviews daily/weekly credit extension/write off reports for unusual or suspicious activity	Supervision

Customer invoice prepared for incorrect amount (5.0)	Occasionally conduct tests of sales order processing accuracy with simulated or historical sales order data	Verification
Customer does not receive invoice (6.0)	Contact customer regarding unpaid A/R balances	Verification
Insufficient inventory to fill customer sales order (7.0)	Periodic audits of database records against actual inventory quantities	Verification
Wrong goods/incorrect quantity picked and packed (7.0)	Review contents against packing slip to ensure correct goods/quantities are picked from inventory	Supervision, records and documentation
Fulfillment center staffers remove goods for personal use/gain (7.0)	Security cameras monitor activity in inventory warehouse; fulfillment center managers or team leaders monitor packers' activities	Supervision

Did you identify similar hot spots and internal controls? Your professor and you can discuss other ideas you included in your table.

Using the ASSRAV toolkit, opportunities to misuse and steal resources (inventory and cash) can be reduced and internal control of these assets tightened. Do you remember the Fraud Triangle and Fraud Diamond introduced in Chapter 2? If people inclined to commit fraud are under pressure or are greedy and can rationalize their behaviors, we can perhaps deter their movements by removing opportunities to act on those impulses. Removing and reducing the opportunity for fraud – as well as decreasing someone's capacity to carry out the fraud – can be accomplished when you employ a strong collection of internal controls.

Before we conclude our discussion of the sales and order fulfillment subprocess it is necessary to talk about potential internal control weaknesses related to setting up new customer accounts. Suppose Bardia is contacted by a new customer, Lewis Medical Supply. Lewis purchases pharmaceutical products for resale primarily to nursing homes and sub-acute care rehabilitation centers. Imagine you are the Bardia sales representative working with the Lewis purchasing agent. What internal controls should be in place at Bardia to deal with new customer account applications? To help you answer this question, consider two significant risks related to doing business with a new customer:

- setting up a fictitious customer
- non-payment by the customer

What data would you ask for in deciding whether to grant credit (*i.e.* set up an account receivable) for a new customer? STOP. Find a partner and take a moment to jot down a brief list. Don't read on until you've completed your list. Remember, this information is going to serve two purposes for Bardia Pharmaceutical. While it's needed for accurate billing and accounting, the information also provides the input for an important internal control – independent verification. Your primary internal control objective is to deter or detect a fictitious customer – and avoid future problems of non-payment – though the credit application task.

How about incorporating the following practices and internal controls into the new customer application process?

- Asking for a street address if customer provides only a post office box number

- Requiring customer to give names and contact information for several trade (business) references

- Asking for the customer's bank information

- Verifying owner or manager details provided on the credit application

- Requiring basic business identifying data (for example, tax and license numbers)

- Conducting independent confirmation of company and financial information provided on the credit application

Safeguarding assets, one of the four objectives of a system of internal control, is at the core of these controls. Inventory and accounts receivable (and subsequently, cash) are the assets Bardia would want to protect. If Bardia can reduce the potential of taking on a fictitious credit customer at the application phase, it improves the chances of making sales on account to legitimate clients and minimizes future inventory losses and bad debt write-offs.

Chapter Core Question 2: How does data flow through the accounts receivable and cash receipts subprocess and what are the internal control vulnerabilities in this subprocess?

Accounts Receivable and Cash Receipts Subprocess Data Flows and Internal Controls

These components of the sales business process focus on activities that occur after the sale. Using the scenario established in the previous section, imagine Bardia Pharmaceutical sold products to Lewis Medical Supply on account. What kinds of activities would affect the Lewis account? Don't forget, we're talking about post-sale activities.

A couple of transactions necessitate updating the Lewis A/R subsidiary ledger by Bardia: Lewis returns some or all of the products it purchased or is granted a sale allowance because of some minor problem with the delivery; and Lewis makes a payment on account. To formulate a stronger understanding of what takes place, let's have a look at the data flow diagrams for both of these common activities of the accounts receivable and cash receipts subprocess. But first, find your partner and try your hand at drawing these two physical DFDs (sales return and allowances, cash receipts). Try not to look at Exhibits 5.2 and 5.3 until you've completed your flowcharts.

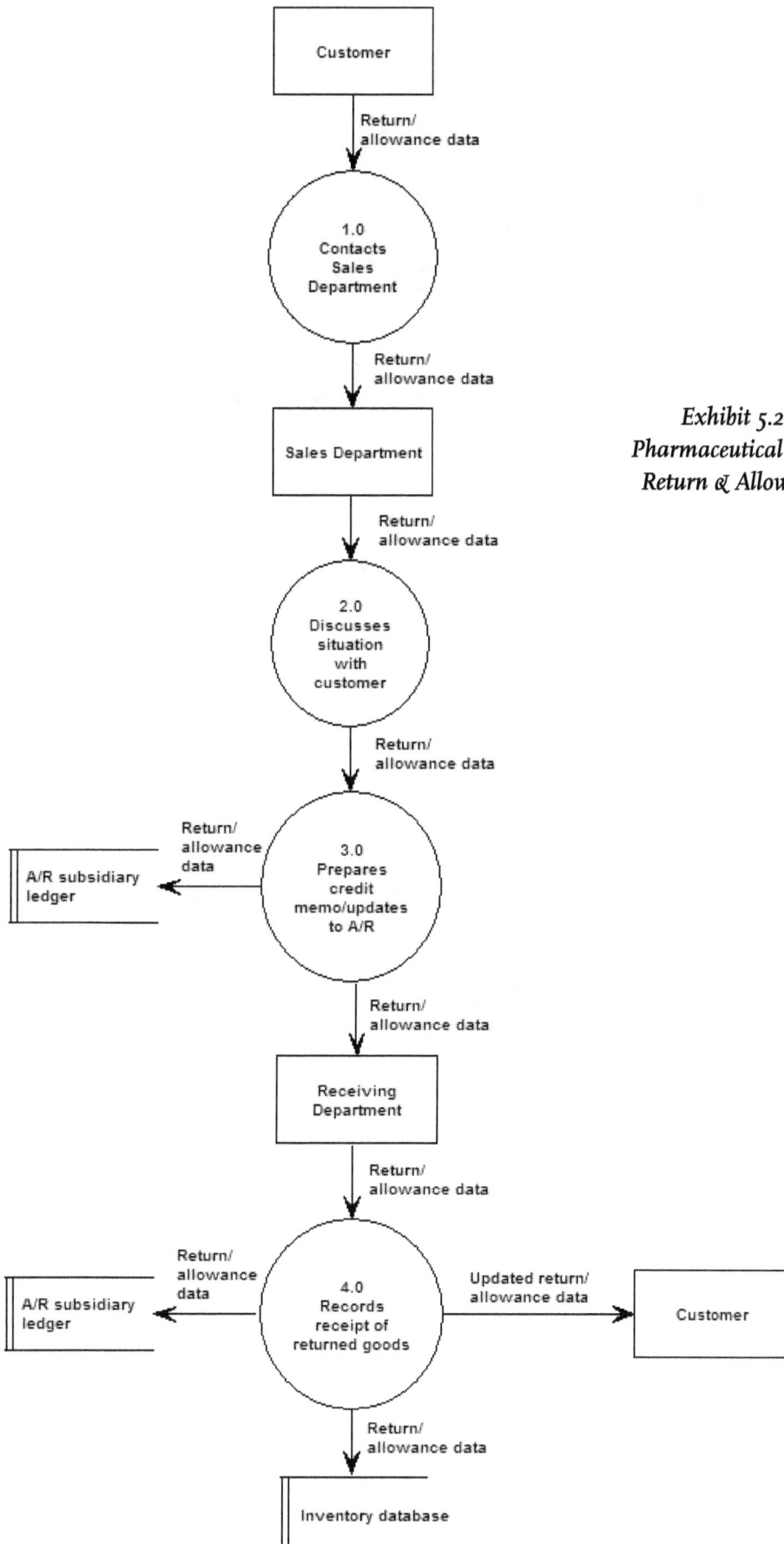

Exhibit 5.2 – Bardia Pharmaceutical DFD for Sales Return & Allowance Activity

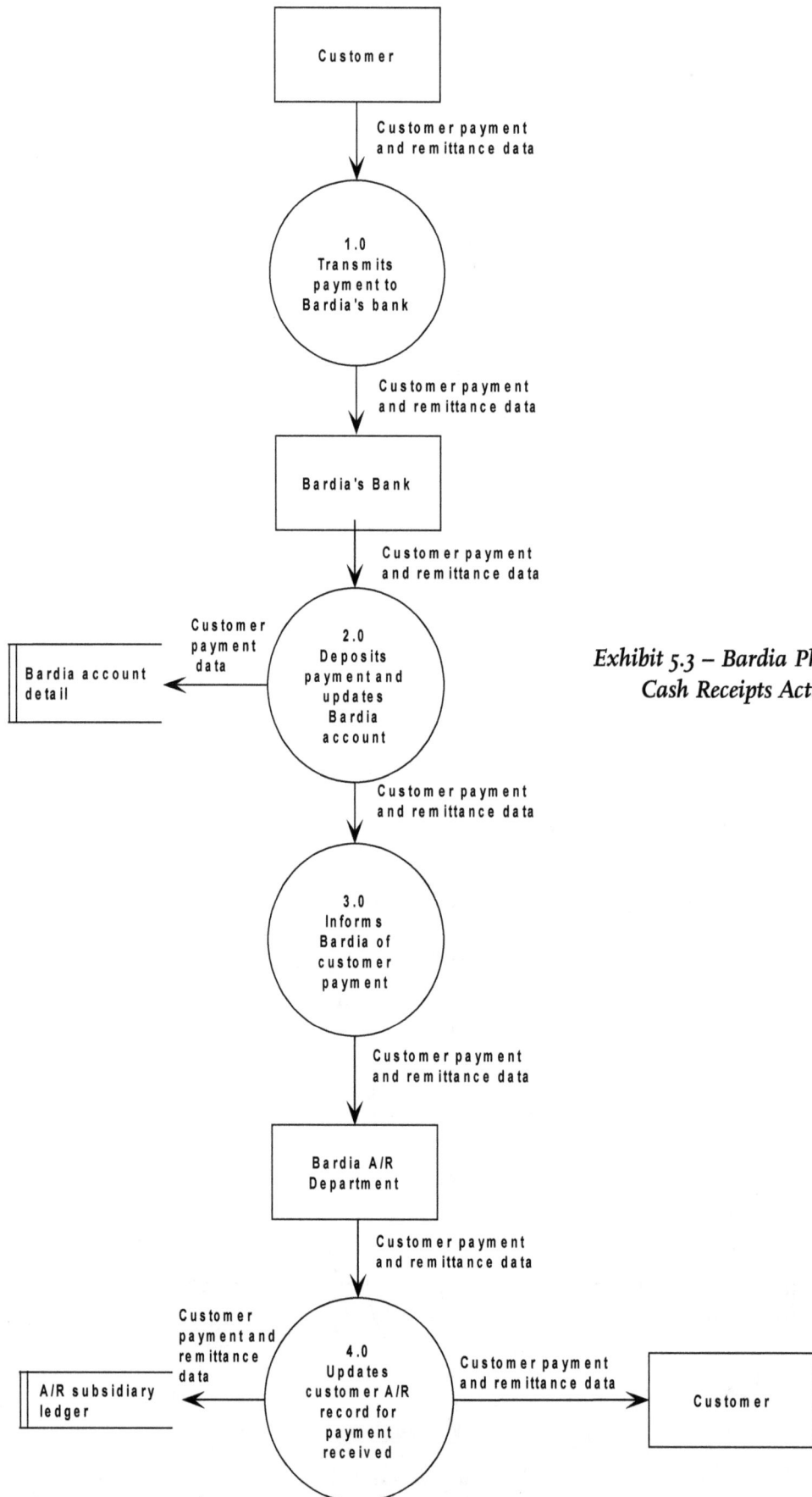

*Exhibit 5.3 – Bardia Pharmaceutical's
Cash Receipts Activity DFD*

Cash Receipts Activity DFD

Do your flowcharts depict similar steps and transactions as those in Exhibits 5.2 and 5.3? Let's review what would be a general set of activities in the accounts receivable and cash receipts subprocess.

Accounts Receivable Tasks and Internal Control Vulnerabilities

This activity, as mentioned in a previous section, would be affected by returns and allowances. What would likely happen when a customer wishes to return goods or be given a sale allowance?

1. Lewis Medical Supply (customer) contacts sales department of vendor (Bardia) to describe rationale for goods' return or sale allowance.

2. Bardia sales department representative reviews situation and decides how to handle return or allowance.

3. Bardia updates customer A/R balance to reflect credit for sales return or allowance.

4. Bardia notifies receiving department about the upcoming product return.

5. Upon receipt of customer's returned goods, receiving department updates inventory records and customer account.

6. Customer receives confirmation that Bardia received returned goods.

In studying the DFD for returns and allowances (Exhibit 5.2) can you identify some potential internal control weak spots? What aspects of this activity might be susceptible to abuse and error? Certainly, each step along the way presents an opportunity for a dishonest sales or receiving department staffer – or a customer – to perpetrate fraud for personal gain. Collusion between two parties can cheat Bardia out of products and cash. The internal controls suggested here can help deter inappropriate actions and safeguard Bardia's assets and help ensure the production of accurate accounting records.

Potential Weak Spots (Process No.)	Suggested Internal Control	ASSRAV Tool
Customer submits false claim for sales allowance (2.0)	Periodic review of customer A/R to uncover patterns of frequent requests for sales allowances	Verification
Customer submits false claim for sales return (2.0)	Require customer to physically return goods, receiving department to inspect/ substantiate returned goods, do not credit A/R until confirmation of goods' return is obtained from receiving department	Verification Records and documents
Sales department issues excessive credit to A/R for customer returns and allowances (3.0)	Supervisor or manager periodically reviews credit memos to detect potential abuses of returns and allowance practices	Verification

| Receiving department reports inaccurate goods return data (4.0) | Receiving staffer doesn't receive customer return data and must count/record returns data independently; accounting software reconciles quantities with customer data provided in process 3.0 | Records and documents, verification |

Cash Receipts and Weaknesses in Internal Control

In medium-sized and larger entities, customer payments on account typically bypass the vendor's place of business. How is that possible? One of two cash receipt techniques would likely be used: a **lockbox system** or **electronic funds transfer** (EFT). In our Lewis Medical-Bardia Pharmaceutical scenario, we can be pretty confident that either method is used.

Whether Bardia uses the lockbox or EFT method, staffers in its accounting department won't handle the customer receipts. Therefore, the data flow diagram in Exhibit 5.3 commences with the customer submitting its hard copy payment (paper check) or an EFT to Bardia's bank.

1. Customer (Lewis Medical Supply) submits paper check or EFT to Bardia's bank.

2. Bardia's bank receives customer payment and remittance data (customer name, account number, and payment amount).

3. Bank updates Bardia's account to show deposit/receipt of customer's payment on account.

4. Bank notifies Bardia it collected customer payment on behalf of Bardia.

5. Bardia updates its A/R subsidiary ledger to acknowledge receipt of customer payment.

6. Bardia confirms receipt of payment on account with customer.

What are the opportunities for error or misuse of assets in the cash receipts activity? View Exhibit 5.3 again and see if you can target a few internal control weaknesses. Because of the strict internal controls employed at financial institutions, many entities face fewer risks when they channel their cash receipts through lockbox systems or implement EFT cash receipt procedures. Nonetheless, several vulnerabilities are present and can be limited with a few well-positioned internal controls.

Potential Vulnerabilities (Process No.)	Suggested Internal Control	ASSRAV Tool
Bank transmits incorrect customer account number to Bardia (3.0)	A/R software matches bank's data against Bardia's valid customer account numbers	Verification
Bardia credits incorrect amount to customer A/R record (4.0)	Daily balancing/reconciliation of customer payments against bank's records of customer cash receipts	Verification

Can't Bardia's bank be the source of some of the internal control problems? Of course it can. But consider this: how can Bardia impose controls on its bank's operating procedures? While another entity is deeply involved in the cash receipts subprocess, Bardia can only exert control over its own tasks and steps. In working with its bank on customer cash collections, Bardia should question its bank about the internal controls in place and satisfy itself that those controls are effective. But Bardia cannot design, implement, and monitor the internal controls of another entity. That is why our list of possible internal control weaknesses only addresses those at Bardia Pharmaceutical.

Reviewing and Glancing Forward

The sales business process is important to for-profit entities since it is the source for the revenues they earn. Effective internal controls are needed in this business process – as well as all others – to promote accurate transaction processing, maintain reliable accounting records and databases, and safeguard the core assets related to the process (inventory and cash).

In the sales and order fulfillment subprocess it is imperative to correctly handle customer orders. Entities need to ensure the products are on hand and that their staffers pick, package, ship, and invoice them without error. Updating customer accounts receivable for returns and allowances can lead to potential abuses, so internal controls are needed to deter and detect opportunities for fraud.

Cash is the most liquid asset and must be protected from theft. In working with cash receipts, one of the strongest internal controls is to reduce the number of people coming in contact with them. Lockbox systems and electronic funds transfer can aid entities in this endeavor.

Next, Chapter 6 takes you through the activities and internal controls of a business process that is central to the activities of all entities: the supply chain business process. From purchasing to payables to cash disbursements, we'll examine subprocess steps, data flows, and internal controls.

Chapter Core Vocabulary

Business processes – coordinated sets of tasks and practices to carry out daily business activities.

Electronic data interchange (EDI) – the paperless, electronic means of communicating standard transaction data between business partners.

Electronic funds transfer (EFT) – a paperless, electronic method for transmitting payments between entities.

Lockbox system – a means of receiving customer payments on account where the customer mails the payment to the vendor's bank instead of the vendor.

Sales business process – the collection of subprocesses related to the revenue earning process. These encompass sales and order fulfillment, and accounts receivable and cash receipts.

Author's note: starting with Chapter 5, the Read It, Do It section contains a capstone minicase that incorporates concepts introduced in the chapter. Students and faculty might use these minicases for in-class exercises, homework, or review.

Read It, Do It – Celebrations LLC

Objectives

To identify internal control strengths and weaknesses in sales and accounts receivable, and recommend ways to reduce these weaknesses.

To understand how adequate accounting records, supervision, and communication can enhance sales and accounts receivable internal controls.

Introduction

Owned and operated by Enzo Nascimento, Hallie Rutledge, and Barbara Wright, Celebrations LLC is an event management and consulting firm. The firm's main office is located in downtown Chicago; two other offices in Schaumberg and Naperville, Illinois, serve corporate and individual clients in the greater Chicagoland area.

Event management is a growing business. When organizations like Motorola, Sears, or the American Bar Association want to host special events for employees, vendors, or members, Celebrations plans, organizes and manages the events. Celebrations also works with individuals for private party planning and management. Clients can select from a number of service options available from Celebrations and choose their level of involvement in planning and running the events. Celebrations' fees depend on the extent of the services provided.

Sales

When a corporate or individual client requires Celebrations' services, the client calls a toll-free phone number and speaks to an event consultant. The first thing the consultant does is to create a client record in Celebrations' client database. This record contains essential information such as the client's name, address, affiliation, classification (individual or corporate client), and billing data. After the client record is established, the consultant and client discuss the event. The consultant makes suggestions about the type of services Celebrations can provide. If the event is large or complex – particularly with corporate events – the consultant works with Enzo, Hallie, or Barbara for suggestions and advice. Once the event plan is worked out, the consultant enters the event's location and agreed-upon services into Celebrations' event order system. From this, an event timeline and planning guide is generated for the consultant and a client invoice produced. Celebrations recognizes revenue immediately, since it considers event planning to be the most significant service it provides to its clients. However, the firm waits until after the event before mailing the invoice to its client.

Accounts receivable

Lately, this practice of recording sales and accounts receivable has proved to be somewhat troublesome. Celebrations recently hired some new event consultants and their estimates of event services have come in lower than what was actually used to run the events. When this happens, Barbara Wright (owner, consultant, and the firm's chief financial officer) updates the invoice to reflect the actual services provided, then reprints the invoice. Her administrative assistant mails the updated invoice to the client. Because invoices are generated, printed, and mailed by each Celebrations office, sometimes the original invoices have already been mailed to clients. Updated invoices often reach clients after the clients have already paid the original invoices. Clients haven't been happy about receiving what they perceive to be "duplicate" invoices, and do not pay them. Now, several clients have past due balances. When these clients subsequently contact Celebrations for services, the consultants remind them about the past due balances. Clients are confused and the consultants sense the clients' negative feelings about Celebrations' inability to keep accurate records.

Required

Please prepare a PowerPoint presentation that: (a) identifies the internal control strengths and weaknesses at Celebrations; and (b) suggests ways to reduce these weaknesses.

Chapter 6

Supply chain business process: purchasing; accounts payable and cash

Chapter Core Questions

1. How does data move through the purchasing subprocess and what are some internal control weaknesses associated with purchasing?

2. What are the common data flows and internal control vulnerabilities in the accounts payable and cash disbursements subprocess?

Introduction

The Tennessee summer afternoon was hot and humid. A hazy sky welcomed visitors to Kingfisher Marina & Resort. Standing at the big picture window in her office, Nancy Kerns, Kingfisher's general manager, smiled as she watched kayakers and fishermen on Kingfisher Lake. Her smile faded, however, as her thoughts turned to tomorrow's meeting with Arun Maghes, audit manager at Srinivasan & Pappas, CPAs. Kingfisher is a new audit client for the firm. The S&P team recently completed the annual audit and Maghes asked to talk with Kerns about weak internal controls in several accounting subprocesses. Nancy knew the accounting department had problems in the past but she thought Kingfisher's new accounting manager, Mark Bednar, had implemented changes in purchasing and accounts payable practices. Apparently he hadn't. Particularly weak were the controls in purchasing, accounts payable, and cash disbursements – those activities making up part of the **supply chain business process**.

Why is it necessary to have a clear flow of data through the supply chain? Many daily decisions depend on having accurate and timely data for inventory, parts and components, and the supplies used to carry out an entity's day-to-day business operations. Whether thinking about inventory levels and sales or the quantities of cleaning supplies available to the janitorial staff, those responsible for monitoring the volume of these items and purchasing them in appropriate amounts need to rely on the data reported in the accounting information system. Acquiring inventory, parts, materials, and supplies results in an expense being recognized (cost of goods sold, various operating expenses) so it also benefits the entity to correctly collect and process this expense data. Can you remember the definition of expenses from your work in introductory financial accounting and intermediate accounting?

"Expenses are outflows or other using up of assets or incurrences of liabilities (or a combination of both) from delivering or producing goods, rendering services, or carrying out other activities that constitute the entity's ongoing major or central operations."[21]

Chapter 6 investigates the movement of accounting data through the supply chain business process, starting with the purchasing subprocess (inventory, materials and supplies) and finishing with the accounts payable and cash disbursements subprocess. To understand supply chain data flows and internal control hot spots we will study the environment at the Kingfisher Marina & Resort. We'll make use of data flow diagrams to lead you through typical data flows and identify some internal control caution points. Are you ready?

Chapter Core Question 1: How does data move through the purchasing subprocess and what are some internal control weaknesses associated with purchasing?

Purchasing Subprocess Data Flows and Internal Control Hot Spots

Before we begin our study of the purchasing subprocess, let's think about how Kingfisher Marina & Resort conducts its purchasing activities.

Kingfisher Purchasing Subprocess Description

Dave Carson is Kingfisher's purchasing clerk. Dave has worked at Kingfisher for 17 years, first as a mechanic at the marina, and then in the housekeeping and maintenance functions. When the former purchasing clerk retired, the accounting manager wanted to replace her with someone who had a detailed knowledge of watercraft and physical plant operations. Dave applied and was chosen for the job.

Weekly, Carson walks around the marina to determine stock levels for a variety of marine supplies, engine parts, and other watercraft-related merchandise. He prepares a **purchase order** and faxes or phones the order to **vendors** in the area. Most of these vendors are the same ones that Kingfisher used when Dave worked at the marina more than 12 years ago. Carson is friends with several of the owners of these companies and occasionally receives holiday turkeys and hams and summer fishing trips to Lake Erie as business gifts. He takes advantage of online purchasing for certain types of marina supplies that are harder to obtain locally. Additionally, Dave makes office and janitorial supply purchases from the online retailers. He makes these purchases under his name and uses his personal credit card. Whether purchases are made through local vendors or online, all goods are delivered to Carson at Kingfisher Marina & Resort.

STOP. Find a classmate and prepare a physical data flow diagram of the purchasing subprocess at Kingfisher. After you've prepared the DFD, identify some of the internal control weaknesses of the purchasing subprocess. Don't read on until you've finished this assignment!

21   Statement of Financial Accounting Concepts No. 6, *Elements of Financial Statements.* Paragraph 80. Financial Accounting Standards Board. Norwalk, CT. December 1985. Available at: http://www.fasb.org/pdf/aop_CON6.pdf

Exhibit 6.1 – Kingfisher Marina & Resort Purchasing Subprocess DFD (Current)

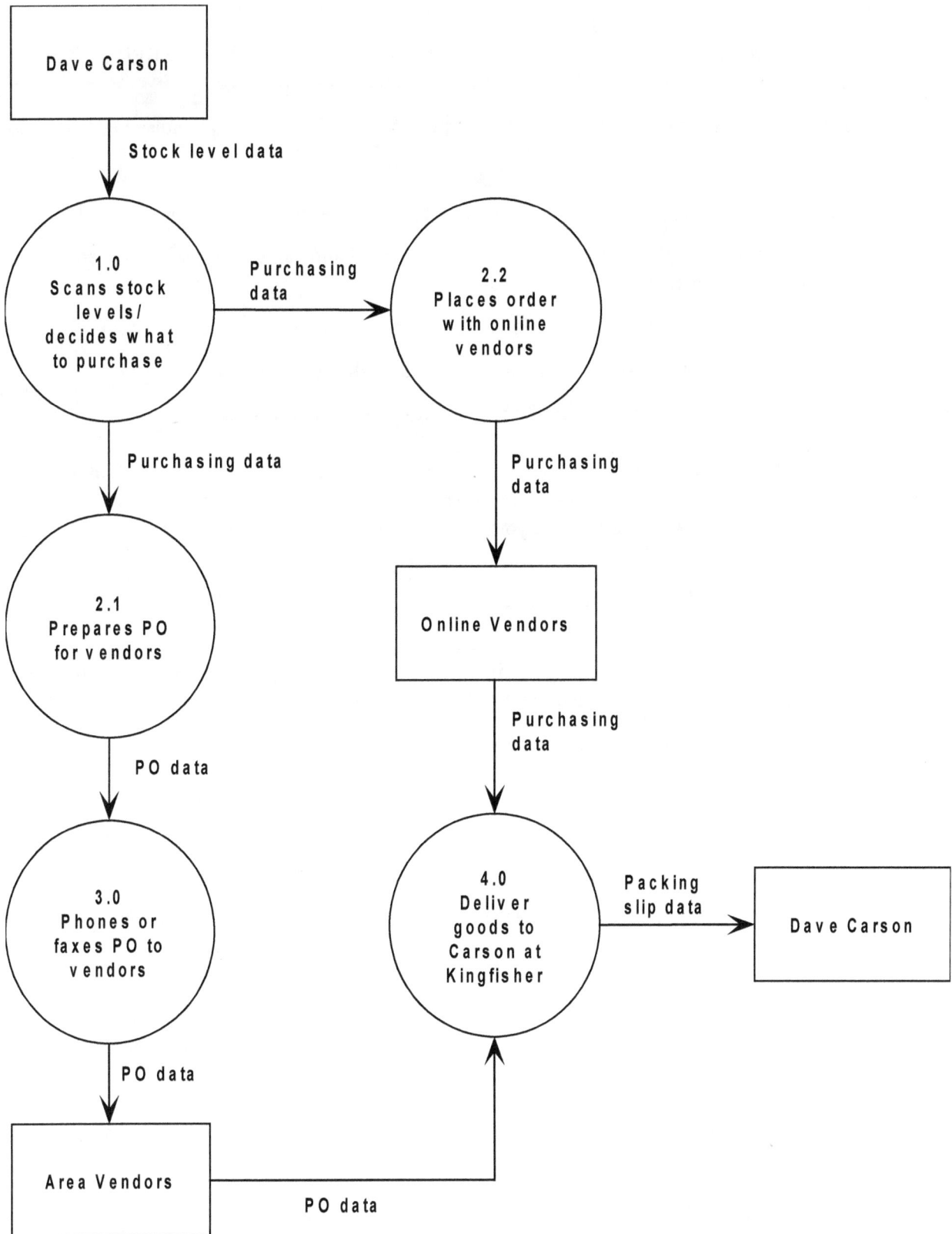

Purchasing Subprocess DFD (Current)

Does your data flow diagram resemble the one above? Remember to reflect both physical and online purchasing methods.

Now how about that log of internal control weaknesses? It's likely to be longer than the DFD itself, isn't it? Here is a non-inclusive list of the problems with Kingfisher's purchasing subprocess:

1. Carson walks around the marina to determine which parts, supplies, and merchandise need to be purchased.

2. Purchase orders are not authorized.

3. Compared to faxed POs, phoned-in orders are susceptible to recording errors by the vendor.

4. Some vendor business gifts given to Carson are substantial and can create real or perceived conflicts of interest in vendor selection.

5. Carson makes online purchases using his name and pays with his personal credit card.

6. It is unclear if online purchases are supported by a Kingfisher purchase order.

7. Carson prepares the POs, places the orders, and takes receipt of goods.

What internal controls would you institute to deter purchasing fraud and mistakes? For each of the weaknesses in the above list, identify a control to reduce the threat and link the control to your ASSRAV toolkit. Format your response in a table. Once you've finished your work compare your ideas to those shown in the table below.

Weakness	Internal Control Suggestion	ASSRAV Tool
1	Maintain perpetual or periodic inventory systems for more accurate purchasing data	Records & documentation
2	Have accounting manager approve purchase orders	Authorization
3	Where practical, fax POs to vendor	Records & documentation
4	Institute policy to limit dollar amount of vendor gifts received, perhaps $50, or even prohibit receipt of vendor gifts	N/A (Policies are part of the *COSO Framework* control environment)
5	Purchases should be made in name of Kingfisher and corporate credit card or corporate account be used for payment	Asset access restriction, records & documentation
6	POs should be prepared for all purchases	Records & documentation
7	Have goods delivered to someone other than purchasing manager	Separation of duties, asset access restriction

Keeping records of parts, materials, and supplies allows Dave Carson to make more accurate purchasing decisions. It will discourage over- or under-buying items, conserving Kingfisher's cash for use where it is more immediately needed. It will be best if these records are maintained electronically, whether using the Kingfisher integrated accounting information system or a spreadsheet that Carson maintains himself.

Presently there is no approval or authorization of purchase orders. Why is approval a desirable component of an internal control system? The chance of purchasing unneeded items increases if one staffer handles the authorization, recordkeeping, and asset custody for a transaction. More significantly, it creates an opportunity (recall the Fraud Triangle and Fraud Diamond) for Carson to purchase goods for himself through the online vendors and have Kingfisher pay for them. Having the accounting manager, Mark Bednar, review and sign (authorize) purchase orders adds an element of oversight to the purchasing process and might discourage Dave from engaging in inappropriate purchasing activities.

When orders are phoned to area vendors, there is a possibility that Carson could recite the wrong item number or quantity or the vendors' clerks might misunderstand or write down the wrong order item or quantity. To promote more accurate handling of the purchase order for all parties it is better, where practical, to submit the PO by fax. It still does not eliminate errors that might occur at the vendors' locations, but it enhances the evidence (records & documentation) created for the data transmission on the Kingfisher side of the subprocess.

The topic of vendor gifts is a complicated one. All businesses like to find ways to thank their loyal, frequent clients and ensure they keep these clients. When gifts are small and incidental – a pen, a calendar, a holiday turkey, or a thumb-sized USB storage device – recipients don't mistake the intent of the gift. In the case of Kingfisher's vendor who treats Dave to Lake Erie fishing trips, the gift's value is excessive and might have other implications. Maybe the vendor is persuading Carson to continue to buy materials even when the price of those materials is higher, or the quality lower, than can be obtained from other vendors. Perhaps the trips are a form of blackmail. Maybe Dave and the vendor are illegally colluding to defraud Kingfisher. Or it's possible the vendor and Carson are middle school buddies and the trips are a way to share the fruits of the vendor's personal success with his old friend.

Regardless, avoiding a real or perceived conflict of interest and an appearance of impropriety in purchasing can be achieved through one of two practices at Kingfisher. The entity can prohibit its staffers from receiving vendor gifts or it can impose an upper limit – for example, $50 annually – on the market value of gifts from vendors. This policy would be included in the Kingfisher staffer manual and highlighted during new staffer orientation. Additionally, the policy might be included in the Code of Conduct that all Kingfisher staffers sign as part of the hiring process.

Although it might be convenient, there are two problems when Dave places online orders using his name and personal credit card. First, it inaccurately portrays the degree of purchasing activity at Kingfisher and misstates detailed accounting data used by Kingfisher managers for operating decisions. Second, Carson could be ordering items for his use and disguising them as Kingfisher purchases. Two ASSRAV tools would enhance internal control over Carson's online purchasing procedures: records & documentation and asset access restrictions. Dave should place orders under the name Kingfisher Marina & Resort, using a business account, so he could have all purchases directly invoiced to Kingfisher. Or if Kingfisher allows some of its managers to use corporate bank cards (such as VISA or MasterCard), Carson should request permission to be issued a corporate credit card. He would use this card rather than his personal card to make online purchases. Either modification would improve Kingfisher's accounting records and data. Having the A/P clerk pay Kingfisher's credit card statement instead of reimbursing Carson (based on amounts reported on his credit card statement) reduces Dave's access to cash.

It is unclear from the purchasing description whether Carson prepares POs for online purchases. If he doesn't, he should. When we review the accounts payable and cash disbursement subprocess in the next section of this chapter you'll see the importance of having corroborating evidence to support paying a vendor **invoice**. At this moment it's enough to say that a PO is needed so Kingfisher's A/P clerk can verify what is invoiced was in fact, requested (ordered).

In a smaller entity it is not uncommon for staffers to perform several incompatible tasks or roles (from an internal control viewpoint). At Kingfisher, Dave falls into this situation. He prepares the purchase order for goods and receives the goods from vendors. How does this weaken internal control? It increases the opportunity for Carson to order items for personal use and take delivery of these items. No one else is involved in the activity so he could easily cover his inappropriate action to avoid suspicion by others. If items are delivered first to Kingfisher's mailroom or receiving center, a staffer independent of the purchasing transaction can indicate what's been received (this data is prepared using a **receiving report**), then take the items to the office that ordered them. This receiving report, along with a copy of the purchase order prepared by Carson, would be sent to Kingfisher's A/P clerk. You'll find out why in the next section.

Chapter Core Question 2: What are the common data flows and internal control vulnerabilities in the accounts payable and cash disbursements subprocess?

Data Flows and Internal Controls in the Accounts Payable and Cash Disbursements Subprocess

Before you read on, please make a list of the tasks and activities related to accounts payable and cash disbursements. Organize them in a logical, sequential order. Does your list resemble this one?

1. Receive vendor invoice.

2. Match data on vendor invoice with purchase requisition (if used), purchase order, and receiving report.

3. Investigate and resolve invoice discrepancies.

4. Schedule invoice for subsequent payment, taking into consideration purchase discount dates.

5. Place unpaid invoices in "unpaid invoice" file according to date.

6. On payment date, retrieve invoice and supporting documentation from unpaid invoice file.

7. Indicate account number(s) and amount(s) to be debited.

8. Send invoices and support documents to appropriate accounting manager for disbursement approval.

9. Prepare checks manually or through payables/disbursements module of the AIS.

10. Deliver checks to authorized individual(s) for signature.

11. Signed checks returned to A/P.

12. Mark invoice and supporting documentation "paid" (date, amount, check number).

13. Mail checks to vendors.

14. File paid invoices and supporting documents in "paid" vendor file according to vendor name.

How would this be depicted in a data flow diagram? Please draw one that depicts the 14 tasks listed above. Don't look at Exhibit 6.2 until you've completed your flowchart.

Exhibit 6.2 – Accounts Payable and Cash Disbursements Subprocess DFD

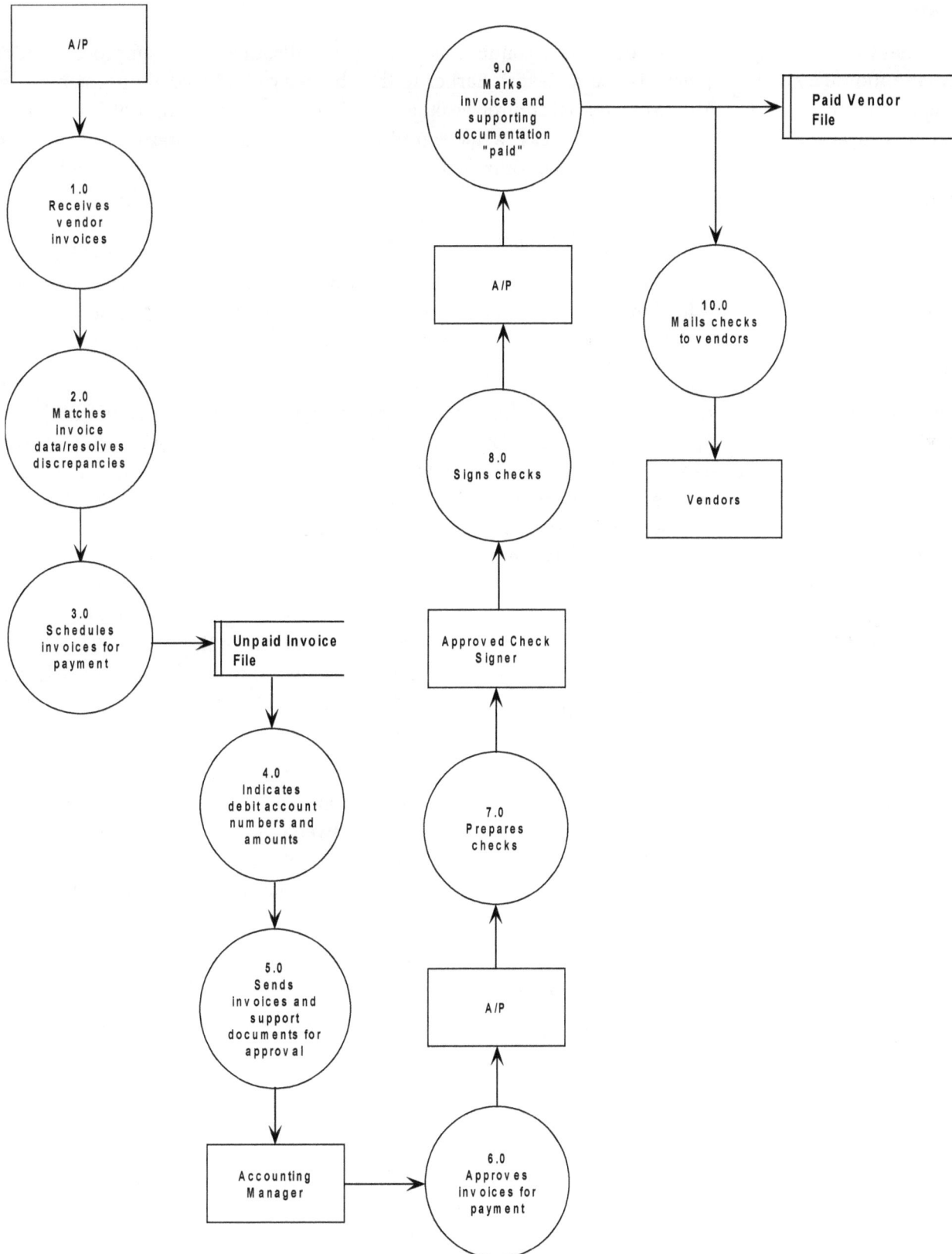

Disbursements Subprocess DFD

How does your DFD compare to the one in Exhibit 6.2? You might have drawn process circles for each of the 14 steps listed on page 74, but it's okay to combine some of those sequential and related tasks into a single process circle.

Now that you've had time to think about the accounts payable and cash disbursements subprocess, let's turn our attention back to Kingfisher Marina & Resort. Earlier in the chapter you learned about the entity's purchasing subprocess and identified its internal control weaknesses. Here's the narrative describing Kingfisher's accounts payable and disbursements subprocess. While you read, make a list of the internal control hot spots and think about the ASSRAV tools and internal controls that could be employed to deter, detect, and limit problems at Kingfisher.

Kingfisher Accounts Payable and Disbursements Subprocess Description

Irene Hohman, Kingfisher's accounts payable clerk, was hired by Kingfisher Marina & Resort after she graduated from Kingfisher High School in 1967. A loyal long-term employee, Hohman has not missed a day's work because of sickness since 1995. She even comes into the office during her vacations to sort through the mail and pick up A/P checks to hand-deliver to local vendors.

Irene receives most vendor invoices through the mail. Some local vendors leave their invoices with her when they deliver inventory and supplies to Kingfisher. For the online purchases he makes, Dave Carson gives Irene his personal credit card statement each month. Hohman writes checks once each week. Every Thursday she gathers all invoices that have arrived since the previous Thursday. She looks over the invoices to make sure they are correct. With nearly five decades' experience at Kingfisher, Irene knows the business's needs inside and out. She uses small business accounting software to prepare the checks. On Thursday afternoons she brings the checks to the accounting manager (Mark Bednar) for his signature. Checks in excess of $2,000 require a second signature. When Hohman receives the signed checks from the accounting manager on Friday morning, she pulls out the checks requiring a second signature and brings them to Nancy Kerns (Kingfisher's general manager). Checks are mailed on Friday around noontime. On her way to the post office or during her lunch hour, Irene sometimes stops at local vendors' offices to hand-deliver their A/P checks. When she returns, she stamps all invoices "paid" and files them according to vendor name.

Before we consider the vulnerabilities in these areas we should acknowledge the strengths of the subprocess. First, checks are written weekly. This frequency allows Kingfisher to take advantage of any purchase discounts offered by vendors without requiring Hohman to write checks in between her usual Thursday disbursement days. While this practice doesn't fit neatly into our ASSRAV internal control toolkit, we can link it back to one of the goals of internal control: promoting the achievement of management's goals and objectives (which includes enhancing operating efficiency).

Another strength is that Irene reviews invoices for correctness. This verification of mathematical accuracy as well as scanning for the reasonableness of the invoice can alert Hohman to potential errors or problems with invoices. Third, Kingfisher uses accounting software to prepare its A/P checks. Records and documentation are strengthened when software is employed, permitting data to be entered once and pulling that data into various modules as needed without re-keying.

Next, checks are signed by someone other than the person preparing checks. Asking the accounting manager and general manager to review and sign checks improves internal control since it adds additional authorization and verification dimensions to the payables and disbursements subprocess. Fifth, dual signatures are required for large dollar disbursements. If the check preparer and check signer were working together to embezzle from the entity, the second signer is in a position to make inquiries about these large disbursements. That person's independent nature and lack of involvement in the supply chain business process encourages inquiry about and/or verification of the disbursements. Finally, invoices are marked so they cannot easily be mistakenly paid a second time. Records and documentation are strengthened since the chance of double-paying an invoice can be reduced when the original invoice is marked "paid". The marking should be large and cover a significant portion of the invoice, making it difficult to alter with a scanner or photocopier to create an "unpaid" invoice that could be used for a duplicate vendor payment.

And what about Kingfisher's internal control weaknesses? Examine this table and see if your list of vulnerabilities and suggested controls is similar.

Weakness	Internal Control Weaknesses	ASSRAV Tool
I	Paying Dave Carson's personal credit card bills for items purchased for Kingfisher	Records & documentation (require Carson to use Kingfisher corporate credit card)
2	Extent of matching invoice data is unclear; no POs or receiving reports seem to be prepared/used	Authorization, verification, records & documentation (regularize use of POs, receiving reports optional)
3	Accounting manager (Bednar) has possession of checks overnight	Asset access restrictions (checks should be locked overnight in a cabinet or safe)

Let's consider the first weakness. As we already explained, there are a few threats to internal control when a company allows its employees to use their personal credit cards when making business purchases. When Dave Carson presents Irene Hohman with his monthly credit card statement, how does she know which items on the statement need to be reimbursed? There's no clear indication – based solely on vendor name – whether a charge belongs to Dave or Kingfisher. Records and documentation (evidence needed for an audit) suffer, too, as purchase orders and receiving reports for these items may not exist. Carson could claim to be buying goods and supplies for the marina when in fact they are personal purchases.

Kingfisher has two choices: it can apply for a corporate credit card and give one to Carson to use for online purchases or it can apply for a business customer account with each online vendor. The more expedient path would be to give Dave a corporate credit card (other Kingfisher managers who frequently make purchases also can be given cards). A similar difficulty exists, however, as no purchase orders or receiving reports are available to confirm the business purpose of their purchases.

This reminds us of a point raised in Chapter 2 where the topic of internal control was first introduced. Remember our discussion of the cost-benefit principle? We wouldn't spend more money to implement an internal control than the value of the resource we are trying to safeguard. Imagine the following scenario. In an effort to streamline activities in the supply chain business process, an entity decides to issue corporate credit cards to several authorized users. But the entity still requires POs to be prepared, receiving reports filled out, and seeks other evidence that credit cards are used solely for business purposes. Don't the tangible and intangible costs of the added steps seem to outweigh the original benefit of giving the corporate cards to its managers? As we consider ways to ensure Carson uses his Kingfisher credit card responsibly, we also must reflect on the costs and benefits of the internal controls. Implementing too many petty rules and practices can defeat the purpose, causing

> Costs to control should be less than the benefits derived from having the control in place.

staffers to ignore or circumvent the rules. As in most aspects of life, a delicate balance needs to be maintained between too much and too little control.

Now look at the second weakness in the subprocess. Our scenario doesn't go into the level of detail we need (and here's the drawback of written descriptions or minicases) so we don't know if Kingfisher requires POs and receiving reports to be prepared. Maybe they're needed for purchases in excess of a certain dollar amount? Perhaps Carson doesn't prepare them for marina-related purchases, but managers in other areas of the resort fill them out? Our description doesn't mention a central receiving office; it's uncommon for smaller entities to have central receiving facilities. We probably would like to know the answers to a few more questions about the way Irene Hohman looks over the invoices to make sure they are correct. In the absence of these details, we'll mention them here.

If purchase orders and receiving reports are used at Kingfisher, Hohman should match the data on all documents. What was ordered should be received, and the same items and quantities should be invoiced by the vendor. When there are discrepancies, Hohman needs to follow up with the Kingfisher staffer who ordered (and received) the items to understand why the vendor invoice reflects different data. As well, the vendor must be contacted particularly if the error or problem is on the vendor's side and needs to be corrected in the vendor's records. Once the discrepancy is resolved, notes should be made on the invoice about the resolution. This provides adequate evidence (an audit trail) for anyone wanting to understand what happened.

What if Kingfisher doesn't regularly use purchase orders or require receiving reports to be prepared when goods are received from vendors? Policies need to be developed to deal with this weakness. Internal controls should be applied consistently across Kingfisher's various divisions. Perhaps thresholds can be established: items costing less than $50 would not require a purchase order. Receiving reports for fixed assets must be filled out. This is a good conversation for Nancy Kerns, Mark Bednar, and Arun Maghes (the external auditor) to have.

The third weakness in Kingfisher's payables and disbursements subprocess is that accounting manager Mark Bednar retains signed checks overnight. At first it seems appropriate that he keep the checks and return them to Irene Hohman the next morning. However, several opportunities for inappropriate behavior present themselves with this situation. If his office is unlocked and he doesn't store the checks in a locked drawer or cabinet, others can access and steal the A/P checks. Another opportunity for trouble rests with Bednar. With overnight possession of the checks it's possible for him to fraudulently alter dollar amounts or payee names on the checks. If he's in collusion with a vendor, he has the perfect chance to facilitate the fraud, doesn't he?

What ASSRAV internal control tool could Kingfisher adopt to reduce these potential vulnerabilities? As mentioned in the table on page 77, locking the signed checks in a file cabinet or safe can restrict access to the checks; the fewer staffers coming in contact with the checks, the better. And where should the checks be stored? Would Bednar's office or the general accounting office where payables clerk Hohman is stationed offer stronger security? This really is a matter of choice and practicality, but it seems more logical for the locked cabinet or safe to be stored in the accounting office. If Bednar doesn't come to the office on a Friday, it might be more inconvenient to access his file cabinet or the safe. More likely, there would be several staffers working in the general accounting or business office and in the event of Irene's absence (but consider her track record!) they would know where her keys are kept and could gain access to the checks for the Friday second signature and mailing tasks.

Two other situations might raise caution flags for us, but aren't easily categorized into our ASSRAV schema. Some people might be disturbed that Irene Hohman comes to the office during vacations and has not taken a sick day in nearly 20 years. Is it possible that Irene Hohman and some vendors are colluding in a long-term and massive plan to defraud Kingfisher, slowly embezzling funds through a complicated system of phony invoices and cash disbursements? Maybe. And why doesn't Irene mail all vendor payments? Why does she sometimes personally deliver checks to certain local vendors? Is it another tactic to avoid the eyes of certain vendors' office workers? Maybe.

In creating this case I imagined a small entity with a cozy and comfortable work environment and did not want to imply fraud and misdeeds by either Dave Carson or Irene Hohman. But the new auditors or the accounting manager might want to understand why Hohman comes to the office on her holiday time and why she drops off checks during her Friday lunch hour. The appearance of impropriety is raised (a caution flag) and thus it's suitable to inquire about these Kingfisher staffer practices. Asking Irene to mail all checks (a stronger practice in the eyes of the auditors) and reassuring her that she can enjoy her vacation time without coming to the office might be all that's needed. This is not unlike situations you might encounter in the workplace during your internships or entry-level fulltime accounting work. The important action for you as an accountant or auditor is to make inquiries about the caution flags you observe and suggest ways to strengthen controls over daily business activities.

To Conclude

The supply chain business process includes three broad sets of activities: purchasing, accounts payable, and cash disbursements. From acquiring goods and services to paying for them, entities must ensure the existence of appropriate approvals (authorization), reliable evidence (records and documentation), and safeguards for the payables checks (asset access restrictions).

It is important to have authorization over purchase requests, particularly those in excess of a particular dollar threshold. In situations where staffers are free to acquire goods and services (as when using corporate credit cards), subsequent reviews and verification of the purchases are necessary (compensating controls).

Before scheduling any invoice for payment evidence must exist to show the items were received or services were provided. Verifying and matching data reported on purchase orders, receiving reports, and invoices helps promote accurate disbursements for items acquired through the supply chain.

Disbursements, whether in electronic or paper form, need to be reviewed by someone other than the payment preparer (verification). Signatures on checks or releases in an electronic funds transfer system – which in fact are authorizations to release funds to payees – also should be made by someone other than the person preparing the payments. In separating a transaction's authorization, recordkeeping, and custody we strengthen internal controls over the most liquid of all entity resources: cash.

In Chapter 7 our focus turns to the fixed assets business process. We examine the life cycle of fixed assets: acquiring, depreciating, maintaining, and disposing an entity's property, plant, and equipment. Fixed asset data flows and internal control vulnerabilities have some similarities to those described in this chapter, so be ready to extend your thinking from current assets (cash and inventory and supplies) to long-term fixed assets (PP&E).

Chapter Core Vocabulary

Invoice – a document from a vendor showing what was purchased, quantities purchased, and the dollar amount owed to the vendor.

Purchase order – a document created by an entity and sent to a vendor when the entity wishes to purchase inventory, parts, materials, supplies, or capital equipment. It includes a description of the items to be purchased, quantities, and stated/quoted prices.

Receiving report – an internal document prepared to indicate what was received and the quantities received.

Supply chain business process – the collection of activities to evaluate and choose suppliers, manage inventory levels, and ensure timely and accurate delivery and payment of goods from suppliers.

Vendors – entities that provide goods or services for an entity; another name for *suppliers*.

Read It, Do It – Highland County Schools

Objectives

To recognize internal control weaknesses in the purchasing subprocess and make suggestions for improvement.

To understand how authorization, records and documentation, and verification enhance a system of internal control.

Introduction

Lindsey Shepherd is the new treasurer of Highland County Schools (HCS). This school district serves approximately 8,400 students in three high schools, four middle schools, and 12 elementary schools across the county.

Purchasing is not centralized at HCS. While the remaining accounting subprocesses have been computerized, purchasing still is handled manually by each school in the district. The process of ordering routine supplies or school equipment is as follows.

The teacher, janitor, or other staffer writes down the items needed on a sheet of note paper and gives the paper to the school secretary. Sometimes when in a hurry, they merely phone their requests to the school secretary. When enough orders have accumulated, the secretary prepares and faxes a purchase order to one or more of the nine approved vendors for office supplies, equipment or other supplies. Usually, the school principal reviews and signs the PO before it is faxed. The secretary sends a photocopy of the PO to the accounts payable clerk at the HCS business office via the school district's courier, who travels by car between each school and the district office at least once a day to pick up/deliver various documents and other items.

When the purchased items are delivered, the secretary signs for them and distributes them to the requestors. Vendors send their invoices to the HCS district office, where the A/P clerk matches the invoices with the POs on file. Vendor invoices are scheduled for payment on the next A/P payment date, which is the third Tuesday of each month.

You are a senior accounting major and have an internship at the Highland County Schools business office. Shepherd knows the internal controls over purchasing and payables need to be improved and asks for your help. She wants to get a quick overview and understanding of the purchasing process and does not need to read through page after page of narrative describing how things work.

Required

Please draw a document flowchart for Shepherd depicting the current purchasing subprocess. Once you have studied your flowchart, think about the internal control weaknesses in this subprocess. What can HCS do to improve internal controls? Write down your ideas in a brief memo to the treasurer.

Chapter 7

Fixed assets business process: acquisition; maintenance & depreciation; and disposal

Chapter Core Questions

1. What are the common data flows and internal control vulnerabilities in the fixed assets acquisition subprocess?

2. How does data move through the depreciation and maintenance subprocesses and what are the internal control weaknesses connected to fixed asset maintenance and depreciation?

3. What are the potential internal control hot spots for fixed asset disposals and how does the related accounting data move through this subprocess?

Introduction

June 17, 2011. Martha de Souza, business manager of a small luxury hotel in New Orleans, is running late. She passes a local pâtisserie, jumps out of her car, and buys a medium black coffee and a dozen mixed pastries and sweets for her staff meeting. Arriving at the Hotel Carmaux, she tosses the car keys to Victor Lam, the valet parking attendant on duty this morning. De Souza sprints through the busy lobby and into the business office, located to the left of the Palmetto Atrium. Her staffers are already seated around the conference table for their weekly department meeting. De Souza smiles and gently places the box of delectable breakfast items on the sideboard near the table. "I ordered coffee, tea, and juice to be brought over from the restaurant," beams Arthur Trimble, as de Souza sits down in a center seat, her usual place at staff meetings. "And here's today's *Times-Picayune*," he adds, sliding the city newspaper across the smooth surface of the teak conference table.

De Souza quickly glances through the front pages of each newspaper section then sets aside the paper to focus on the agenda of this week's staff meeting: fixed assets. The hotel's owners want to have renovations in the dining room, bar, and café completed in the next two months. De Souza and her staff are responsible for disposing the old furniture and equipment and acquiring the new.

Other discussions completed, de Souza adjourns the meeting and heads to her office, *Times-Picayune* in hand. The headline she didn't notice while quickly scanning the newspaper before the staff meeting now seems to jump off the page: "New Orleans failed to keep tabs on assets in 2009, inspector general says"[22]. She sits back and reads the article:

"In the latest of a series of critical reports about New Orleans' financial and administrative operations during former Mayor Ray Nagin's administration, Inspector General Ed Quatrevaux said Thursday that during 2009, the city had weak controls over its fixed assets, meaning its property, buildings, furniture and equipment.

"Quatrevaux said an audit found that the city bought and disposed of assets without evidence of proper approvals, the same asset was recorded more than once on its books, and the city did not perform annual inventories.

"Without proper controls, for instance, the city has no way of knowing whether it still has all the furniture, computers and other items it has paid for and whether they are in usable condition.

"The report notes that the 2009 audit report by the city's external auditors, the firm of Postlethwaite & Netterville, also found that the city 'did not have adequate policies, procedures and internal controls in place to ensure all capital assets were fairly stated in its financial statements on a timely basis.'

"The inspector general's audit 'revealed that certain components of the city's fixed-asset internal control processes were ineffective, which could create an opportunity for' significant errors in its financial statements, the report says. 'The city had several policies in place outlining fixed-asset controls; however, the policies failed to address timely recording, notification of additions and disposals, tagging and inventory requirements'."

De Souza makes notes of the city's fixed asset internal control weaknesses and photocopies the article to distribute to her staff. It will serve as a good reminder of the significance of following internal control policies and practices.

Accurate accounting for an entity's property, plant, and equipment (PP&E) is important for several reasons. First, as noted in the *Times-Picayune* article, PP&E amounts reported on the balance sheet should be trustworthy and reliable, reflecting a believable quantity and quality of the fixed assets owned and in use by the entity. Second, achieving management's goals and objectives is made easier when working with carefully assembled data. And because fixed assets can represent a significant proportion of an entity's long-term assets, safeguarding PP&E is a responsibility of all staffers.

Chapter 7 emphasizes the data flows and internal controls typically in place for an entity's property, plant, and equipment. Commonly called the **fixed asset business process**, accounting for long-term physical assets can be viewed from the perspective of a *life cycle*. First, the assets are acquired. Then they are depreciated over their useful lives. Throughout their useful lives they might be improved or enhanced so the cost of any capital expenditures must be tracked and added to the assets' original costs. Finally, assets will be selected for trade-in, sale, or another form of disposal (*e.g.* donation) and the accounting data related to these dispositions must be removed from the ledger.

Before we turn to the chapter's core questions, let's recall the nature of fixed assets:

"Property, plant, and equipment typically consist of long-lived tangible assets used to create and distribute an entity's products and services and include land and land improvements, buildings, machinery and equipment, and furniture and fixtures."[23]

---

22   Eggler. B. "New Orleans failed to keep tabs on assets in 2009, inspector general says". The Times-Picayune, June 17, 2011. Available at: http://www.nola.com/politics/index.ssf/2011/06/new_orleans_failed_to_keep_tab.html

23   ASC 360-10-05-3. Property, Plant, and Equipment. Norwalk, CT: Financial Accounting Standards Board, 2013.

Inventory and fixed assets differ primarily in that inventory represents assets acquired specifically for resale to customers. Fixed assets are an integral part of an entity's business operations and not intended to be sold to customers.

Chapter Core Question 1: What are the common data flows and internal control vulnerabilities in the fixed assets acquisition subprocess?

Data Flows in the Fixed Asset Acquisition Subprocess

Imagine you are Martha de Souza. Over the next two months you're overseeing the PP&E disposals and acquisitions for the hotel dining room, bar, and café. How do you suppose the PP&E acquisition subprocess should function at the Hotel Carmaux? STOP. Find a classmate and list the steps you believe are appropriate for this activity. Continue reading only after you completed your list.

1. Dining room, bar, and café (DBC) managers work with interior designer and select furniture and equipment.

2. DBC managers or business office staffer prepare purchase orders for vendors (interior designers specify vendors to be used).

3. De Souza or Hotel Carmaux general manager approves POs.

4. Business office staffer sends POs to furniture and equipment vendors.

5. Vendors deliver furniture and equipment to Hotel Carmaux.

6. Business office staff place **fixed asset ID tags** on furniture and equipment.

7. Business office staff enters fixed asset ID data into spreadsheets or fixed asset module of accounting software.

8. Summary data from fixed asset ID tags shared with accounts payable clerk.

9. Invoices received from vendors.

10. Accounting manager periodically reconciles general ledger fixed asset account balances with fixed assets subsidiary ledger account balances.

Some variation would exist in the way entities handle their fixed asset acquisitions. But authorizations, records and documentation, and independent verification are important internal controls that must be included in the acquisition subprocess. In the next section we will discuss internal controls over PP&E acquisitions. For now, let's stay focused on the way fixed asset data moves through the accounting information system.

What would a physical data flow diagram look like for the steps described above? With your partner, sketch the DFD. Don't look ahead until you've finished your flowchart.

Exhibit 7.1 – Hotel Carmaux Fixed Assets Acquisition Subprocess DFD

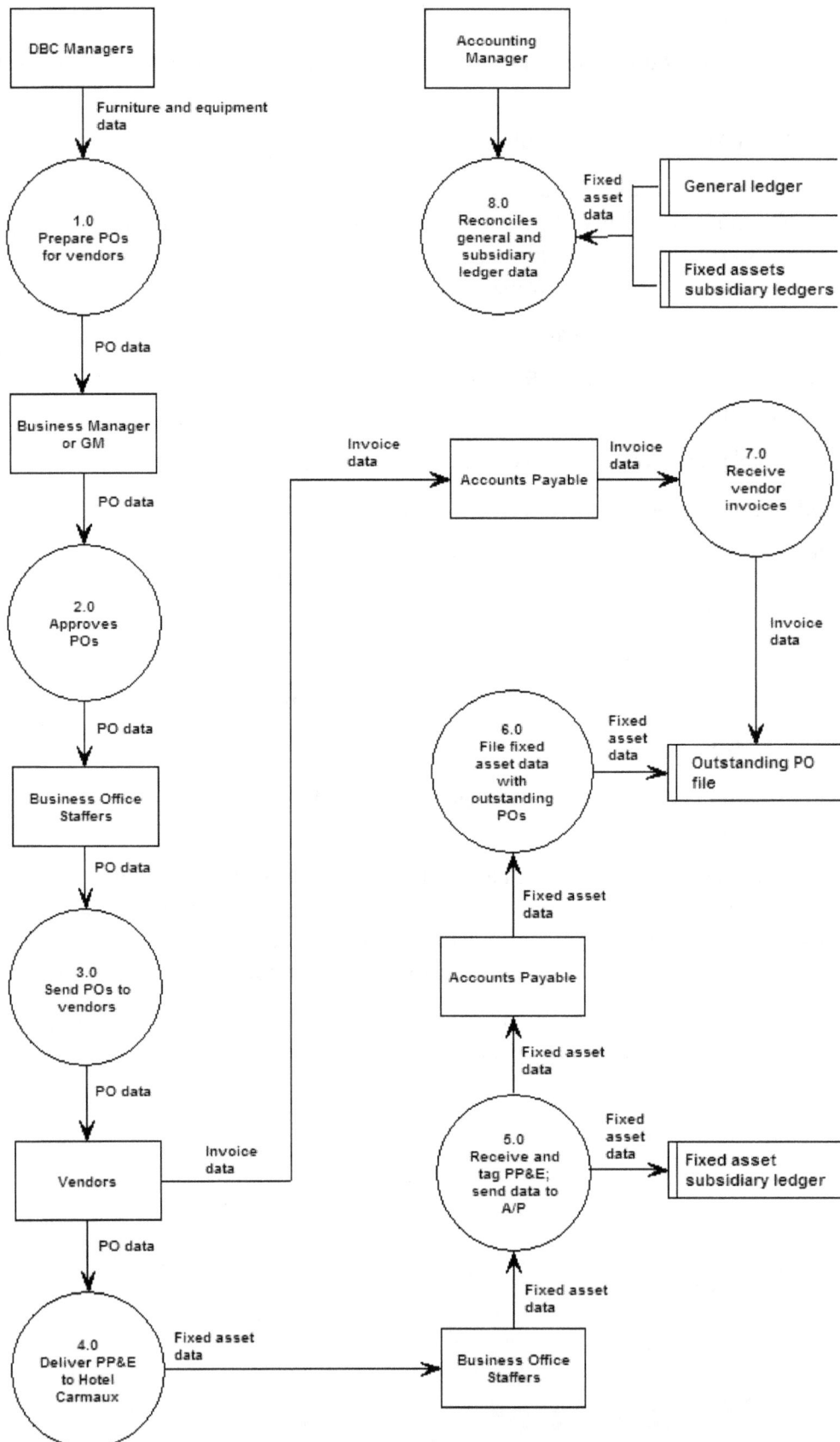

Acquisition Subprocess DFD

Does your data flow diagram look somewhat like the one in Exhibit 7.1? Remember, we can combine several closely related tasks into one process circle to reduce the size of the DFD.

This data flow diagram communicates the first phase of the life cycle of fixed assets: acquisition. Now let's turn to the internal control vulnerabilities associated with acquiring property, plant, and equipment.

Internal Control Vulnerabilities of the Fixed Asset Acquisition Subprocess

Martha de Souza, after reading the newspaper article about the city's fixed asset internal control problems, visits the Office of Inspector General's website. She downloads the June 2011 report and reviews it. De Souza identifies several key internal control breaches for fixed asset acquisitions. These include:

1. Fixed assets acquired without proper approvals.

2. Fixed assets not always recorded when received.

3. The same assets erroneously recorded multiple times.

4. Fixed assets not identified with unique identification tags[24].

With the upcoming renovations and higher than normal levels of fixed asset purchasing activity at the Hotel Carmaux, de Souza wants to be sure that the risk of such vulnerabilities will be minimal. What internal controls should be in place for PP&E acquisitions? STOP. Find a partner, talk about the question, and draft a list of internal controls you'd put in place (and identify the related ASSRAV tool) to reduce the incidence of problems like those that affected the City of New Orleans. After you develop your list, review the table, below. There should be similarities between the two sets of suggestions.

Weakness	Internal Control Suggestion	ASSRAV Tool
1	DBC managers, de Souza, and hotel general manager must approve fixed asset acquisitions	Authorization
2	When fixed assets are delivered, paperwork (bill of lading, shipper's documents) sent to business office and data entered into fixed asset spreadsheet or accounting system; copies of paperwork given to A/P clerk	Records & documentation, verification
3	Paperwork identified in (2) above is marked "received" and dated to reduce situations of multiple entry of same asset data	Records & documentation
4	Affix ID tag immediately upon unpacking fixed assets; record asset location and other data in fixed assets subsidiary ledger/fixed assets module in accounting system	Records & documentation, verification

24 Office of Inspector General, City of New Orleans. City of New Orleans Fixed Asset Internal Control Performance Audit. June 16, 2011. Available at: http://www.nolaoig.org/uploads/File/Audit/fixed%20assets%20final%20report.pdf

These internal controls should help the Hotel Carmaux from suffering the same problems with which the city was plagued. Introducing better recordkeeping, updating the records in a timely manner, and adopting multiple levels of authorization for fixed asset acquisitions will strengthen the hotel's accounting for PP&E. De Souza and her staff, as well as the hotel's general manager, must carry out their responsibilities during this period of increased PP&E transaction activity. Accurate financial reporting, safeguarding the new fixed assets, and ensuring that the hotel management's goals are met all depend on the diligence of those involved in each step of the process.

Chapter Core Question 2: How does data move through the maintenance and depreciation subprocesses and what are the internal control weaknesses connected to fixed asset maintenance and depreciation?

Fixed Asset Maintenance and Depreciation Subprocesses Data Flows

After the furniture and equipment are delivered, set up, and installed at the Hotel Carmaux, these fixed assets enter the second phase of their life cycle. The depreciable cost of PP&E will be allocated to expense over their useful lives. Management choice affects depreciation calculations. Management must agree on appropriate useful lives (in years or productive capacity) and residual values; these decisions directly impact the amount of depreciation expense reported on the income statement. We will revisit the impact of such choices when we discuss the internal control matters connected to fixed asset depreciation and maintenance.

And what's the significance of management choice on fixed asset maintenance? The principle aim of this question isn't about decisions of timing (for example, to perform maintenance on the stoves and ovens in fiscal year 2014 or 2015). Rather, the emphasis is on how to categorize the maintenance costs. Think back to your introductory financial accounting course. Do you remember the distinction between revenue expenditures and capital expenditures? If costs to improve a fixed asset significantly extend its useful life or materially alter the way the asset will be used, how should these costs be recorded? GAAP requires them to be capitalized and subsequently depreciated. Otherwise, costs for routine maintenance and repair (upkeep) of PP&E should be expensed when incurred. In the next section we will identify potential internal control hot spots related to the revenue v. capital expenditure decision.

Can you envision the accounting data flows for the depreciation and maintenance subprocesses? STOP. With a classmate or two, draw the physical DFD for these activities. After you finish your flowchart, examine Exhibit 7.2 and observe similarities and differences in your and this DFD.

Exhibit 7.2 – Hotel Carmaux Fixed Assets Maintenance and Depreciation Subprocesses DFD

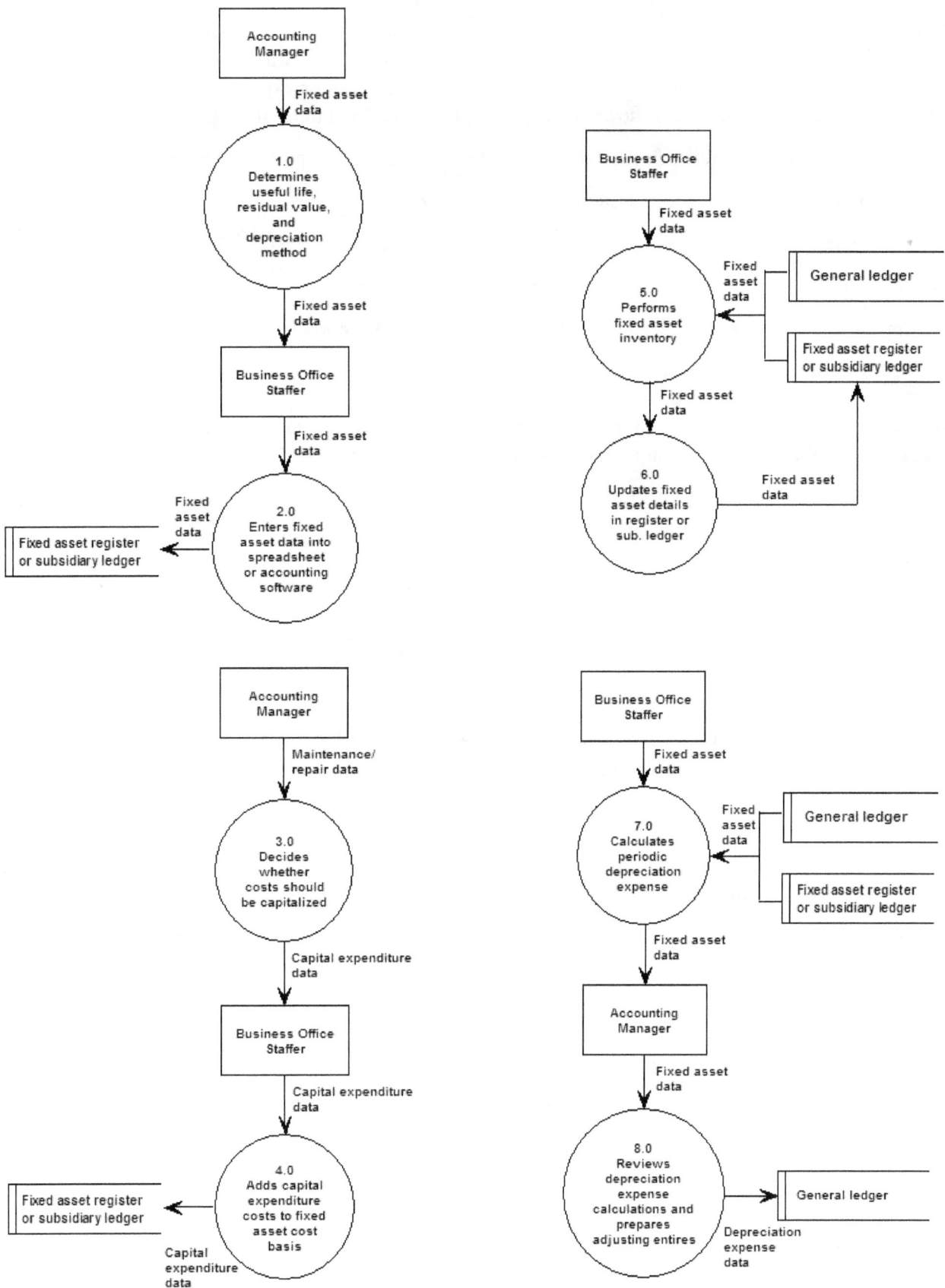

Maintenance and Depreciation Subprocesses DFD

In contrast to some of our other physical data flow diagrams, the flowchart in Exhibit 7.2 presents four discontinuous tasks: entering depreciation characteristics into the fixed assets register/accounting module when the asset is first acquired; updating the fixed asset records for capital expenditures; performing the periodic fixed assets inventory; and calculating periodic (quarter or annual) depreciation expense. Therefore, the DFD doesn't strictly adhere to the fundamental flowcharting practices we outlined in Chapter 3.

Internal Control Vulnerabilities in the Fixed Asset Maintenance and Depreciation Subprocesses

Let's revisit the four objectives of a system of internal control:

- safeguard entity resources;

- encourage production of accurate accounting records and related statements;

- promote achievement of management's goals and objectives; and

- ensure conformance with external regulators' rules.

Martha de Souza goes back to the inspector general's report on internal control weaknesses. What does she read related to the fixed asset maintenance and depreciation subprocesses?

1. The City didn't employ useful asset descriptions, stopping auditors from properly identifying assets.

2. The City and its sub-units failed to conduct inventories of their fixed assets.

3. The City lacked controls to properly classify repairs and maintenance expenses[25].

De Souza is determined not to let the Hotel Carmaux's fixed asset activities be subject to the same level of recklessness as was the city's. She meets with her accounting manager, Arthur Trimble, to review and revise their internal controls.

STOP. Find a partner and role play the discussion between de Souza and Trimble. In addition to the weaknesses identified in the inspector general's report, can you think of potential flaws connected with the maintenance and depreciation subprocesses at the Hotel Carmaux? Jot down a list of these hot spots. Once you finish making your list, read on.

In addition to the internal control hazards mentioned in the inspector general's report, several maintenance and depreciation activities are vulnerable to error and manipulation, as enumerated below:

1. Unnecessary maintenance might be performed.

2. Maintenance could be undertaken by unskilled staffers.

3. PP&E useful lives and residual values could be inappropriate.

4. Depreciation might be incorrectly calculated.

5. Depreciation on some fixed assets could be overlooked.

---

25 Ibid.

How would these vulnerabilities affect internal control if left unaddressed? The first, unnecessary maintenance being performed, is a hot spot because it wastes staffer time (increases payroll expense) and cash. One of the objectives of a system of internal control is to safeguard assets. The most liquid of all assets, cash, is wasted when unneeded repairs and maintenance are carried out.

How is internal control threatened when maintenance is performed by unqualified staffers? Two internal control objectives are at risk: safeguarding assets and ensuring management's goals and objectives are being met. When someone lacking proper training attempts to repair or maintain a fixed asset there's a chance the work will not, in fact, fix the problem. The hotel will need to contact a credentialed technician – which it should have done from the outset – and waste time and resources in the process. The PP&E and cash are wasted or at risk (safeguarding assets), and delays in getting the fixed asset back into working order impacts daily operations and interferes with achieving the hotel management team's goals and objectives.

What's the internal control impact of inappropriate useful lives and residual values for fixed assets? Similar to the situation of incorrectly capitalizing the cost of routine maintenance, there's an effect on the financial statements: too long a useful life and periodic depreciation expense is understated. The reverse is true if the useful life is too short; the amount of depreciation expense recognized in each accounting period is more than it ought to be. And since residual value must be taken into account when calculating depreciable cost, this too can affect the amount of depreciation expense recorded each period. This will taint the internal control objective of producing reliable accounting data and related financial statements.

The fourth and fifth activities noted in the above list have the same impact on internal control as the one just explained. Incorrect depreciation calculations – including omitting some fixed assets from depreciation calculations – will over- or understate periodic depreciation expense and the book value of reported PP&E.

So how do de Souza and Trimble ensure that all fixed assets are identified in the accounting information system, that depreciation is correctly calculated (given accurate depreciable cost data, suitable useful lives, and consistency in applying depreciation methods), and necessary maintenance is being carried out by qualified staffers or independent contractors? Think about the internal controls you'd implement at the Hotel Carmaux if you were Arthur Trimble, accounting manager. Relying on the format we've used for this section of each chapter, please prepare a table noting the recommended internal control along with the related ASSRAV tool. Please don't look ahead until you've written down your ideas.

Weakness	Internal Control Suggestion	ASSRAV Tool
1	DBC managers must approve fixed asset repairs/maintenance; work performed noted in fixed assets subsidiary ledger	Authorization, records and documentation
2	DBC and/or hotel maintenance managers approve work to be done by in-house staff or outside contractors; managers monitor progress/quality of work performed	Authorization, supervision
3	Accounting manager, in consultation with DBC managers, chooses useful lives and residual values for PP&E acquisitions	Authorization, verification
4	Accounting manager scans periodic depreciation calculations for reasonableness; performs analytical reviews of random PP&E transactions	Verification
5	Business office staffers periodically perform fixed assets inventory to determine all are recorded and depreciated	Records and documentation, verification

Finally, what can be done to remedy the three internal control problems mentioned in the inspector general's report? Let's consider the first two problems listed on page 88. It's important to adequately describe your PP&E in the accounting information system so these assets can be quickly and easily identified for ID tagging and subsequent fixed asset inventories.

And the third problem? Ignoring the distinction between capital and revenue expenditures affects the integrity of the Hotel Carmaux's accounting records and related financial reports. When ordinary maintenance and repair costs are capitalized they decrease the reported amount of periodic maintenance expense on the income statement. Consequently, this overstates fixed asset account balances. And in future accounting periods reported depreciation expenses are overstated, thereby understating operating income. Granted, the amounts we are talking about are not material; but one of the objectives of internal control is to produce accurate and reliable accounting records and reports. Misclassifying maintenance costs as additions to PP&E just doesn't represent the transaction faithfully.

It's also useful for details of ordinary maintenance and repairs to be indicated in the fixed asset records. While these costs (revenue expenditures) don't affect PP&E account balances, keeping track of maintenance performed on fixed assets helps managers decide whether additional repairs or capital improvements are needed or if it's time to dispose of the assets.

Many effective fixed asset internal controls depend on staffers who are independent of maintenance and depreciation activities. Those staffers examine, review, or consult with members of the business office. Such controls incorporate another perspective or a staffer not involved with performing the task and permits the action or decision to be reviewed by someone less likely to treat the transaction with a casual carelessness. The result of that additional conversation, explanation, or review just might be the difference between error and accuracy, poor and wise judgment, or innocent mistake and fraud.

Chapter Core Question 3: What are the potential internal control hot spots for fixed asset disposals and how does the related accounting data move through this subprocess?

Fixed Asset Disposals: Data Flows and Internal Control Weaknesses

Martha and Arthur are having a light lunch at the Hotel Carmaux café. They've addressed internal controls for nearly all subprocesses of the fixed assets life cycle. Now it's time to evaluate and modify controls for the last phase of a fixed asset's life: disposals. In fact, the very furniture they're sitting on will be replaced in a few weeks since the café is the first of the three facilities to be renovated. On the back of a paper placemat, Arthur documents for Martha his understanding of the current process for fixed asset disposals. His data flow diagram is shown in Exhibit 7.3.

Disposal Subprocess DFD (current)

Exhibit 7.3 – Hotel Carmaux Fixed Assets Disposal Subprocess DFD (current)

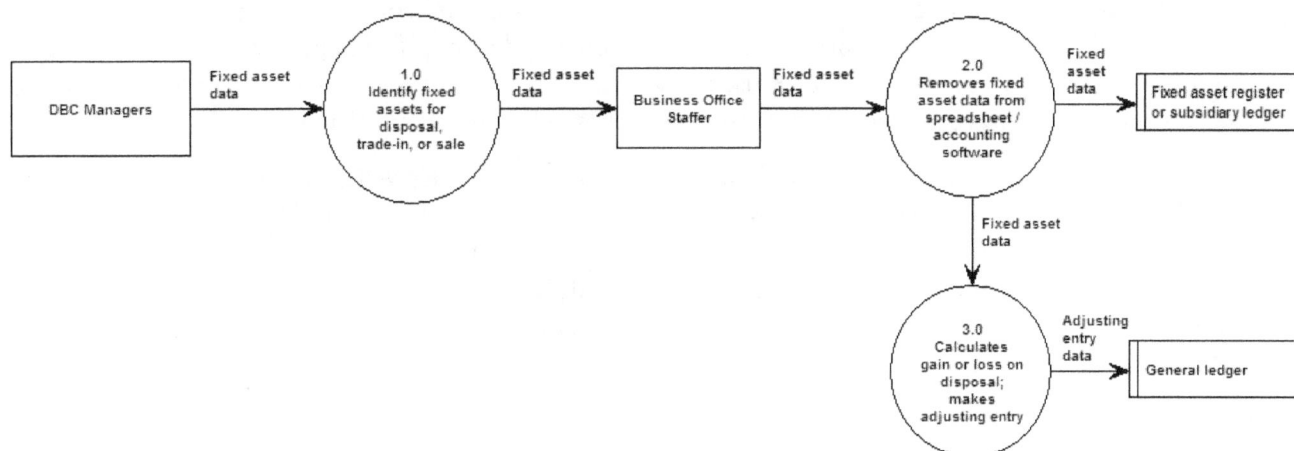

Arthur and Martha glance at the inspector general's report of internal control weaknesses related to asset disposals:

Fixed assets did not have suitable approvals or support before removing them from the fixed asset register[26].

Martha peered over the top of her water glass at Arthur. "You know what this means?", she mused. "Alas, I do," shrugged Arthur. "We have to modify the way we handle disposals around here".

Where are the vulnerabilities in the Hotel Carmaux's subprocess? STOP. Examine the Exhibit 7.3 flowchart and prepare a brief list of weak spots you observe in the PP&E disposal activities. Please don't continue reading until you finish writing your list.

We can identify several trouble spots related to asset disposals from Exhibit 7.3:

1. No business office approval (accounting manager or business manager) needed prior to asset disposition.

2. No verification/evidence that PP&E is actually sold, traded in, sold for scrap, or donated.

3. Fixed asset ID tags not removed/returned to business office before asset disposal.

---

26   Ibid.

So what can de Souza and Trimble do to enhance internal control over property, plant, and equipment disposals? First, they should require staffers requesting disposals to have accounting manager (Trimble) and business manager (de Souza) authorization. A new form needs to be created on which a dining room, bar, or café manager makes the request to dispose of fixed assets under their control. The requester should indicate the reason for and method of asset disposal. The business manager's authorization should be required because she doesn't have PP&E custody or recordkeeping tasks, unlike the accounting manager. This adds a dimension of independent verification to the disposal subprocess. By reviewing and approving the requests, she can determine if the disposals are necessary and evaluate the appropriateness of the planned disposal methods.

How do Martha and Arthur know that assets marked for disposal have actually been sold, traded in, donated, or brought to the salvage/scrap junkyard? Could hotel staffers be taking fixed assets targeted for disposal and bringing them home to furnish their houses or the houses of friends? While it appears okay to allow staffers to take older furniture from the dining room, bar, and café, is it in the best interest of the hotel's owners? Would it be better to trade in, sell, or donate the furniture? This is one reason it's important to have someone independent of the disposal activity to approve it and endorse the disposal method. When the fixed assets are disposed of, we need confirmation that they've reached the buyer, charitable organization, or salvage yard. Acknowledgment by the recipient and a representative from the hotel can be obtained through signatures on a form created for the purpose. Perhaps it can be the same form used to get authorization for the asset disposal. A two- or three-part *fixed asset disposal* form could provide the evidence gathered by these control activities.

The third internal control that should be implemented is to remove the Hotel Carmaux fixed asset ID tag at the time of disposal. The asset ID tag would be affixed to the asset disposal form. When sent to a business office staffer, it offers documentation to remove the asset from the spreadsheet or fixed asset register/module in the hotel's accounting information system. Based on the information that an asset has been sold, scrapped, or donated, the business office staffer or the accounting manager would calculate the gain or loss on the asset disposal and make the journal entry to update the accounts.

As we reflect on the fixed asset disposal subprocess it is important to design a cluster of internal controls that will promote accurate accounting records, encourage a smooth flow of accounting data between the staffers who need it, and provide evidence of the assets' transfer to buyers or charitable entities. At the same time, the controls should not be burdensome to the staff or encourage those bound by them to circumvent the steps because they add seemingly unnecessary work. And the internal controls must always abide by the cost-benefit rule: the cost of implementing the controls needs to be lower than the benefits derived by having them in place.

Summarizing Chapter 7

Through the actual examples from the City of New Orleans and the illustrations of the fictitious Hotel Carmaux, we've been introduced to the fixed asset business process. Made up of three core activities – acquisition, maintenance and depreciation, and disposals – the day-to-day accounting for PP&E depends on an undisturbed flow of data between accounting and business office staffers and those working in other areas of the entity. Authorizations, a separation of duties, trustworthy records and documentation, and verification help strengthen the internal control environment.

Using a made-to-order maker of wood products, Chapter 8 takes you through the data flows and internal controls in the production and manufacturing business process. You'll observe the extent of the connections from sales to supply chain to fixed assets and production/manufacturing processes with the scenario built around Wolf River Hardwoods. Will you be ready to synthesize your knowledge and understanding from Chapters 5, 6, and 7? I hope so.

Chapter Core Vocabulary

Fixed asset ID tags – a flexible plastic, paper, or metal tag affixed to property and equipment specifically identifying the asset. Tags are sequentially numbered, and some may have bar codes to facilitate the fixed asset inventory task.

Fixed assets business process – the collection of tasks to acquire, maintain, depreciate, and dispose of an entity's long-term physical assets.

Read It, Do It – AlloyVend.com

Objectives

To identify internal control weaknesses in a company's fixed assets business process.

To understand how authorization, supervision, independent verification, and accurate recordkeeping can reduce internal control weaknesses.

Introduction

AlloyVend.com was started in 2004 by Noah Jiang, Henry Zhi, and John Liu, former employees of a large multinational aluminum manufacturer. AlloyVend.com pools the trio's 50 years of metals industry experience as well as Henry's recent background as a consultant in IT architecture and security. Within seven months of the site's launch date, AlloyVend.com counts more than 160 metals companies in its client base. The company has added 24 employees to its payroll in the last six months. Many of the company's employees work from home or spend time on the road at client offices, relying on a sophisticated, secure company VPN for doing business. Clients of AlloyVend.com use the company VPN to log into the storefront and auction services, message board, and knowledge databases.

Information Technology (IT) Infrastructure

AlloyVend.com has not been immune to the explosive growth of mobile computing devices attributed to the advancements in wireless technology. Each company staffer is supplied with a smartphone and tablet computer. An open area at the AlloyVend.com headquarters – the bullpen – is a large work space where staff can spend an occasional day at the office or drop in between customer appointments. The bullpen is equipped with laser printers, PC docking stations, and photocopier/scanners. Employees permanently stationed at the AlloyVend.com campus have access to desktop and laptop computers, printers, and scanners.

IT Fixed Assets Policies and Procedures

AlloyVend.com's policy is to expense IT devices costing under $500. Fixed assets costing in excess of this amount, including staffer smartphones and tablet computers, are capitalized and depreciated using the straight-line method over a useful life of three years. The company uses the fixed assets module in its financial accounting software to handle all fixed asset transactions. Renata Carlucci, accounting manager, has overall responsibility for the effectiveness of the company's fixed assets accounting activities. She is not involved with asset selection or evaluation, purchasing, receiving, or maintenance. Rather, Carlucci delegates these activities to the company's Information Technology (IT), Purchasing, and Receiving Departments.

Asset Acquisition

When an employee wants to acquire a new piece of IT equipment or when the company hires new staffers and needs to outfit them with the basic IT resources, current staffers or the human resources manager send an e-mail message to the IT Department. The e-mail message describes the kind of equipment requested and the date by which the assets are needed (typically the new hire's start date). The IT manager decides if the requisition is appropriate, and if so, approves the purchase. She forwards the e-mail to the Purchasing Department, where the purchasing agent searches for the product on the websites of online retailers. The purchasing agent is instructed to purchase from vendors who sell the assets at the lowest price. The purchasing agent prepares and authorizes purchase orders. The purchasing agent faxes the POs to vendors, and sends copies of the POs to the requestor and the Receiving Department.

When assets arrive at AlloyVend.com's Receiving Department, the clerk confirms the information on the PO with the vendor shipping documents packed with the assets. The clerk writes the date the assets were received on his copy of the PO and also makes note of any special situations or asset conditions on the PO. Then, the clerk delivers the assets to the requestors and sends the marked PO to the accounts payable (A/P) clerk. The A/P clerk handles vendor payments for assets in the same manner as other payables, but performs one additional step: she photocopies the vendor invoice and gives it to Carlucci. Carlucci uses this data to create a new fixed asset record in the accounting system.

Maintenance and Repairs

Since the company has such a large number of IT devices and many of the staff do business on the road or from home, managers decided to decentralize responsibility and authority for repairs and maintenance to individual staffers. For example, if a staffer's laptop is not working, he has the authority to contact a local computer repair company for repair or replacement of the device. Sometimes staffers bring their devices to the AlloyVend.com campus and ask the IT Department to examine it or replace it with one of the spare devices kept on hand for emergencies. Staffers generally make payment for these repairs/replacements on their personal credit cards and give their monthly statements along with the repair receipts to the AlloyVend.com payroll clerk. She processes these reimbursement requests once each month. These non-taxable reimbursements are paid at the same time monthly salaries and commissions are paid.

Asset Disposals

When computer and communication devices are retired, traded in, or otherwise disposed of, Carlucci is to be alerted so she can update fixed asset records. In practice, this rarely takes place. The company lacks a well-defined policy about replacing old IT devices. When staffers receive their IT devices it's unclear whether these are part of their compensation package and become their property. Sometimes staffers keep older technology items and give them to their children. There have been several instances where staffers have advertised old smartphones or laptop computers for sale on eBay then keep the cash proceeds from the sales.

The Loan

Jiang, Zhi, and Liu need additional capital to grow the business. They met with a commercial loan officer at their bank, who indicated that audited financial statements are needed before she can evaluate their business loan application. AlloyVend.com engaged a regional public accounting firm for the audit. As part of the pre-audit work an evaluation of internal controls needs to be undertaken.

Required

You are the senior auditor on the engagement. You are getting ready to meet with Renata Carlucci to talk about the internal controls over fixed assets. Please prepare a handout of the key points you plan to discuss with Carlucci: the internal control weaknesses and suggestions for remedying these weaknesses.

Chapter 8

Production & manufacturing business process: scheduling; and production

Chapter Core Questions

1. How does data flow through the scheduling subprocess?

2. What are the internal control weaknesses associated with the scheduling subprocess?

3. What are the typical data flows in the production control subprocess?

4. What are the potential trouble points in internal control for the production control subprocess?

Introduction

Although many commercial and residential construction supply companies have seen a downturn in their business over the last few years, Wolf River Hardwoods has been largely unaffected by the construction slump. You might wonder why. Wolf River produces custom wood products using computer controlled equipment to enhance quality and reduce operating costs. Additionally, Wolf River offers products in a wide price range, allowing customers to choose lower priced wood floors, paneling, and decorative beams when their budgets demand it. Employing fewer than 20 people – most of whom are highly skilled and work in production and manufacturing – Wolf River is lean and effective.

Wolf River operates on a **made-to-order business model.** The company primarily sells to building contractors and interior designers. Once customers place an order – for example, for bamboo kitchen flooring or mahogany paneling – Wolf River sources the raw wood and upon receipt of it cuts, sands, and stains the wood to customer specifications.

Chapter 8 discusses the flow of data across the **production & manufacturing business process.** You also will see the manner in which data from the sales, supply chain, and fixed assets business processes are shared with the production & manufacturing process. Accounting information systems textbooks define production & manufacturing subprocesses in different ways. And this text is no different. In an attempt to keep the process understandable and uncomplicated, we'll divide the process into two major subprocesses: scheduling and production control. Now let's integrate what we've covered in the last few chapters to see what kinds of transactions and internal control hot spots are associated with the production & manufacturing process.

Chapter Core Question 1: How does data flow through the scheduling subprocess?

Data Flows in the Scheduling Subprocess

Bucky Wilson, Wolf River's owner and salesman, hangs up the phone and looks over the notes he made while talking with the project manager at Gallatin Construction. Wolf River has just received a significant order for hardwood flooring that will be installed by Gallatin in a new restaurant and bar. Wilson transcribes the details from his notes onto a purchase order for rosewood, cherry, and white oak timber. Gallatin also will use the wood to craft a custom bar and one-of-a-kind fireplace mantels for the restaurant.

Wilson also serves as purchasing agent for Wolf River. He researches which of his hardwood vendors has the best prices, quality, and availability, then places the orders. Performed simultaneously with ordering, Wilson also considers the supply chain timeline and how it dovetails into Wolf River's production schedule and Gallatin's required delivery date. He works backward chronologically, noting the delivery date to Gallatin, estimating the dates needed for sawing to size, staining, and finishing the hardwoods (and taking into consideration other customer jobs that will be worked on during the same time frame), and fixing the date by which Wolf River needs the raw materials. Based on this date and the vendors' abilities to deliver on according to this timeline, Wilson prepares POs for two vendors. One will source the cherry and white oak lumber; the other vendor will supply the rosewood. Wilson gives copies of the POs to his warehouse manager, Tima Klein, who will match the PO data with the delivery details once the hardwoods are received from the vendors. Purchase order copies also are sent to the A/P clerk. He files these POs in the open PO file.

When the lumber is received from the two vendors, Klein verifies the vendors' shipments are what Wolf River ordered. She makes note of any defects or other problems with the order. Following the data flows described in Chapter 6 (supply chain business process), acknowledgment that the order has been received is sent to Wolf River's accounts payable clerk, Biz Wilson (Bucky's son). He awaits vendor invoices and processes payments in a manner consistent with that outlined in Chapter 6. Biz also handles customer billing (A/R) and uses this same purchasing data when he calculates raw materials costs to be billed to customers.

In addition to contacting the A/P clerk, Klein notifies production manager Steve Sibicky when lumber is received. Sibicky is then ready to review the customer job details with Bucky Wilson and modify, if necessary, the production schedule.

Observe the connections among production, sales, and supply chain business processes. In a small, made-to-order environment steps frequently happen concurrently and it might be challenging to keep staffers in the information loop. STOP. Find a partner and prepare a physical data flow diagram that portrays the production scheduling subprocess at Wolf River. Please don't look ahead until your flowchart is finished.

Exhibit 8.1 – Wolf River Hardwoods Production Scheduling DFD

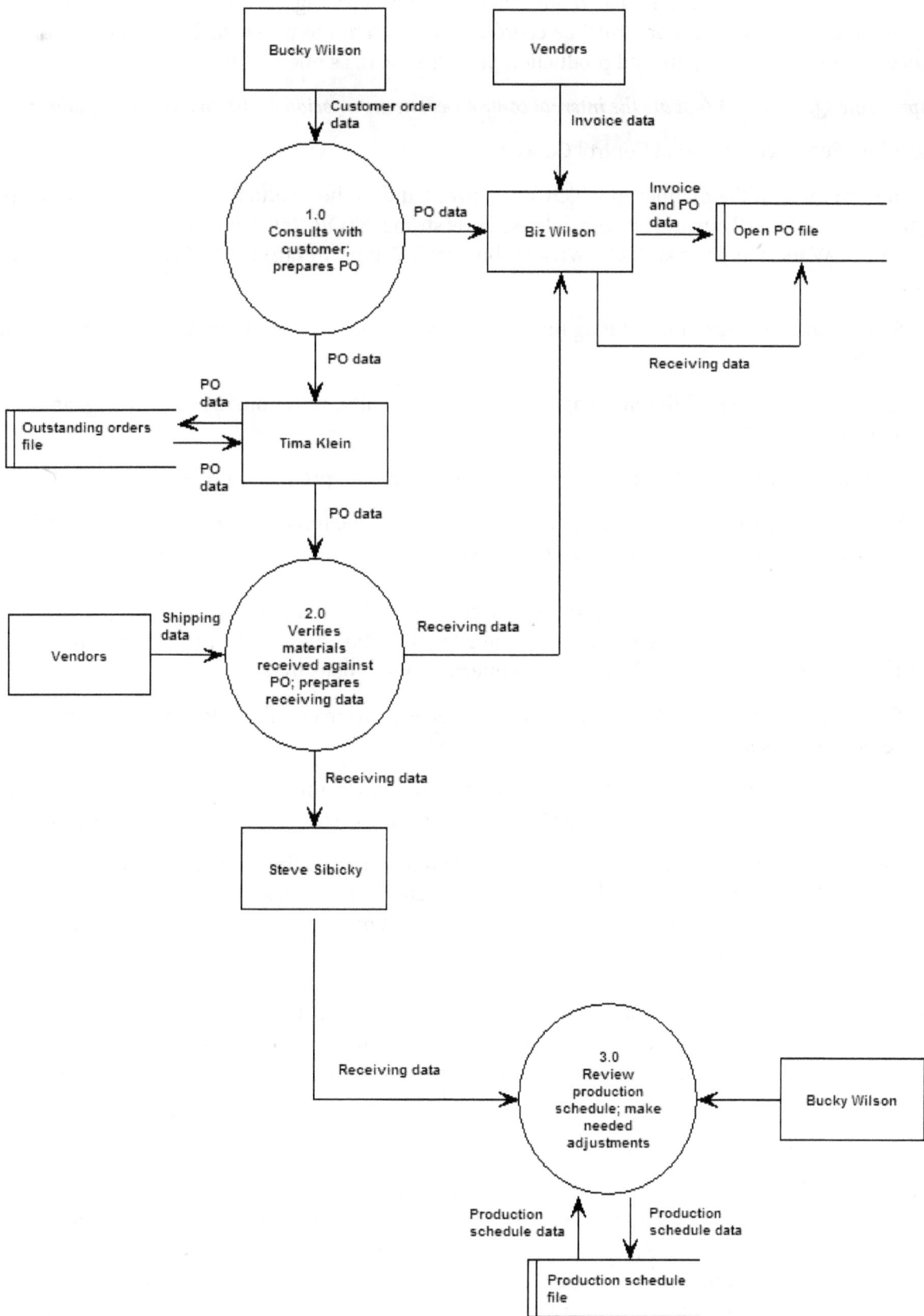

Wolf River's data flows demonstrate the importance of frequent and fluid communications in a custom manufacturing environment. Sales, before it can commit to making and delivering products according to customer deadlines, must discuss raw materials requirements with purchasing and production. Manufacturing schedules for all of the company's work must be coordinated to determine which staffers and pieces of equipment are needed. Sales, supply chain, and production processes work as one unit to serve customers.

Chapter Core Question 2: What are the internal control weaknesses associated with the scheduling subprocess?

Scheduling Subprocess Internal Control Concerns

What do you think of the manner in which Wolf River handles the production & manufacturing scheduling subprocess? For a small business its controls are fairly strong. STOP. Refer to Exhibit 8.1 and make a quick list of the ASSRAV tools in place at Bucky Wilson's business. You may examine the list below after you jot down your ideas.

1. Supervision: production scheduling manager and owner monitor and modify production schedules when needed.

2. Separation of duties: different people perform purchasing, warehousing, disbursing, and scheduling activities.

3. Records & documentation: sales orders, POs, receiving data, production scheduling data are maintained.

4. Verification: A/P clerk matches data from various source documents to ensure accurate vendor invoicing and cash disbursements for purchased raw materials.

Wolf River's strongest internal controls are its separation of duties and evidential support (records & documentation) for transactions. Tasks related to raw materials acquisition and production scheduling are carried out by different staffers. This accomplishes several internal control objectives:

•   Safeguarding resources. Warehouse manager oversees raw materials; A/P clerk doesn't disburse cash to vendors unless purchasing and invoicing data agree.

•   Ensuring accurate accounting data/financial statements. Documentary evidence and independent verification of data improves likelihood that journal entry data is trustworthy and can be relied upon.

•   Promoting achievement of management goals and objectives. Efficient production and keeping customers satisfied can certainly be considered goals of Wolf River's management team; involving staffers from across the business processes increases the chance that potential problems or delays will be spotted and corrective action taken.

But what about the internal control vulnerabilities in the production scheduling subprocess? Can you identify spots where controls might be needed to deter or detect errors or fraudulent activity at Wolf River Hardwoods? STOP. Draft a list of the potential problems and suggest internal controls that could be implemented to deal with those problems. Don't read on until you've completed your list.

There are a couple of hot spots in the subprocess that we might wish to examine.

Internal control weakness A: Bucky Wilson might be steering business to vendors with whom he has a close relationship rather than those offering the best customer value. *Suggestion:* while this is a possibility, it is not likely to occur. Wolf River's warehouse manager, production manager, manufacturing staffers, and customers will notice problems related to inferior quality timber. However, Bucky Wilson should consider developing an approved vendor list from which to source raw materials. This will be particularly useful in circumstances when his usual vendors are unable to supply timber according to his specs or timeline. Additionally, Wilson knows it is not in his long-term interest to harm his company's reputation by procuring timber products merely to benefit his business buddies.

Internal control weakness B: Tima Klein, warehouse manager, could misstate quantities received compared to the actual delivery or report timber quality as unsuitable and divert the raw materials to her benefit. *Suggestion:* another staffer could be given the task of receiving raw materials but what is to stop this staffer from doing the same thing as Klein? What about asking a warehouse or production staffer to be present when Klein receives the raw materials? How do you think this will be interpreted by Klein? And is it a waste of staff time? Unless Bucky Wilson suspects wrongdoing by his warehouse manager, the best control is already in place. Biz Wilson matches PO data, receiving data, and data on the vendor invoice before he pays the vendor. If he observes a pattern of irregularities between vendor invoices and Klein's receiving data he would mention this to his father, who would discuss it with Klein. If Klein was altering raw materials receiving data, the conversation with Bucky Wilson might be sufficient to deter her from perpetuating her theft.

Internal control weakness C: Data in the production schedule file might be erroneous, leading Sibicky and Wilson to overlook production scheduling conflicts. *Suggestion:* as Steve Sibicky enters new data or revises data in the production schedule he can scan it for reasonableness and accuracy before submitting it. Perhaps one of the more experienced production staffers could be brought into the task and asked to review the data. This independent verification might raise questions about staffing, equipment, or raw materials that had been overlooked by Sibicky. Bucky Wilson needs to consider the probability of Sibicky entering incorrect data into the production schedule. But since Wilson reviews the production schedule with Sibicky, it might not be worth pulling a production staffer into the task to provide an additional internal control over data accuracy.

In summary, Wolf River's production scheduling subprocess incorporates internal controls suitable to its business environment, structure, and size. If Bucky Wilson suspects problems, he's in a position to investigate and communicate his concerns with staffers. As an active owner/manager, his presence also serves as an internal control. His is the role of supervisor and verifier of daily work.

Chapter Core Question 3: What are the typical data flows in the production control subprocess?

Production Control Data Flows

It's 4:00pm on a Tuesday, and Steve Sibicky and Bucky Wilson are looking over the next few days' production schedule data. Tomorrow, Wolf River starts work on the Gallatin Construction job. Five days are budgeted for cutting the custom white oak flooring for Gallatin's restaurant client. Sibicky and Wilson review the production staffers who have been assigned to the job, look over the equipment that will be used, and visit the warehouse to examine the white oak timber. They are satisfied with all, and as production for the day is winding down and the daily machine cleaning begins, Sibicky tacks the job assignment directions to the production board located in the production staff meeting room.

6:35am Wednesday. Production staffers start to arrive at Wolf River, suiting up and donning their safety gear in time to begin their shift at 7:00am. Ivan Cedeño has already started brewing pots of regular and decaf coffee in the production staff meeting room. Staffers grab cups of java and doughnuts – brought today by Jenny Livingston, one of Wolf River's master carpenters – then walk over to the production board to see today's work assignments.

Out on the factory floor, Steve Sibicky sends a written **raw materials requisition form** with a list of the raw materials needed for the morning's cutting, including the Gallatin white oak timber. Tima Klein, warehouse manager, receives the requisition form, retrieves the required inventory, and notes the inventory and quantities removed from the warehouse, signs the requisition form, and keeps a copy for her records. The timber and signed materials requisition form are sent to the factory floor where they are delivered to the proper equipment stations and cutting work commences.

Throughout the morning, Sibicky monitors the progress of various cutting jobs on the factory floor, and then swings over to the sanding booth and staining room to investigate the status of those activities. When he encounters staffers having trouble with their work, he assesses the situation and immediately updates the production control database to reflect production delays. This is the data used at the end of each day when Sibicky meets with Bucky Wilson to review daily and weekly production schedules.

As tasks are completed and work-in-process moves from stage to stage, Sibicky updates the production control database. Although perceived by some staffers as unnecessary, the laptop computer, wireless network, and production control database long ago demonstrated their contribution to Wolf River's manufacturing efficiency. Once all work is completed, Sibicky enters this data into the database and also prepares a **finished goods inventory transfer form**. The finished products and the form are sent to the finished goods storage area of the warehouse. Tima Klein indicates receipt of the finished goods on the form, keeps a copy for her files, and sends the signed copy of the finished goods inventory transfer form back to Sibicky. A copy of this form also is sent to Biz Wilson so he can bill customers for work completed.

After lunch, Sibicky submits a raw materials requisition form for the afternoon's production needs. The same process is used by Tima Klein to remove timber from the warehouse and sign off on the materials requisition form. As production staffers position the white oak timber on one of the saws and begin to cut, one staffer senses the unmistakable smell of burning oil. Smoke starts billowing from under saw #3. He throws the emergency kill switch. The staffers working on that saw, plus Sibicky, gather around to inspect what happened. Sibicky calls the maintenance department and one of the machine technicians and the Wolf River electrician hurry down to the factory floor. After 45 minutes of work, the technician tells Sibicky he's going to have to order parts from the saw manufacturer and perhaps have the manufacturer's technician make a service call. Fortunately, Wolf River carries maintenance contracts on all its cutting and sanding equipment. The technician phones the manufacturer and a service call is arranged for Friday. After deciding how to schedule today's unfinished tasks, Steve Sibicky enters the details into the production control database.

The workday's conclusion at 4:00pm arrives all too soon. Bucky Wilson and Steve Sibicky are again meeting to review the next five days' production schedules. Taking into consideration that saw #3 will be out of commission for perhaps three days and juggling delivery dates with some patient customers, they agree on a revised work schedule for the remainder of this week. Sibicky updates the files, prints out tomorrow's assignments, posts the list on the production control board hanging in the staff meeting room, and calls it a day.

At Wolf River Hardwoods and other manufacturers, data flows in the production control subprocess occur mainly within the segments of the production center: factory floor, warehouse, and production managers' offices. Would you like to prepare a DFD of the Wolf River production control process? Find a partner and get to work. Don't look at Exhibit 8.2 until you're finished with your flowchart.

Exhibit 8.2 – Wolf River Hardwoods Production Control DFD

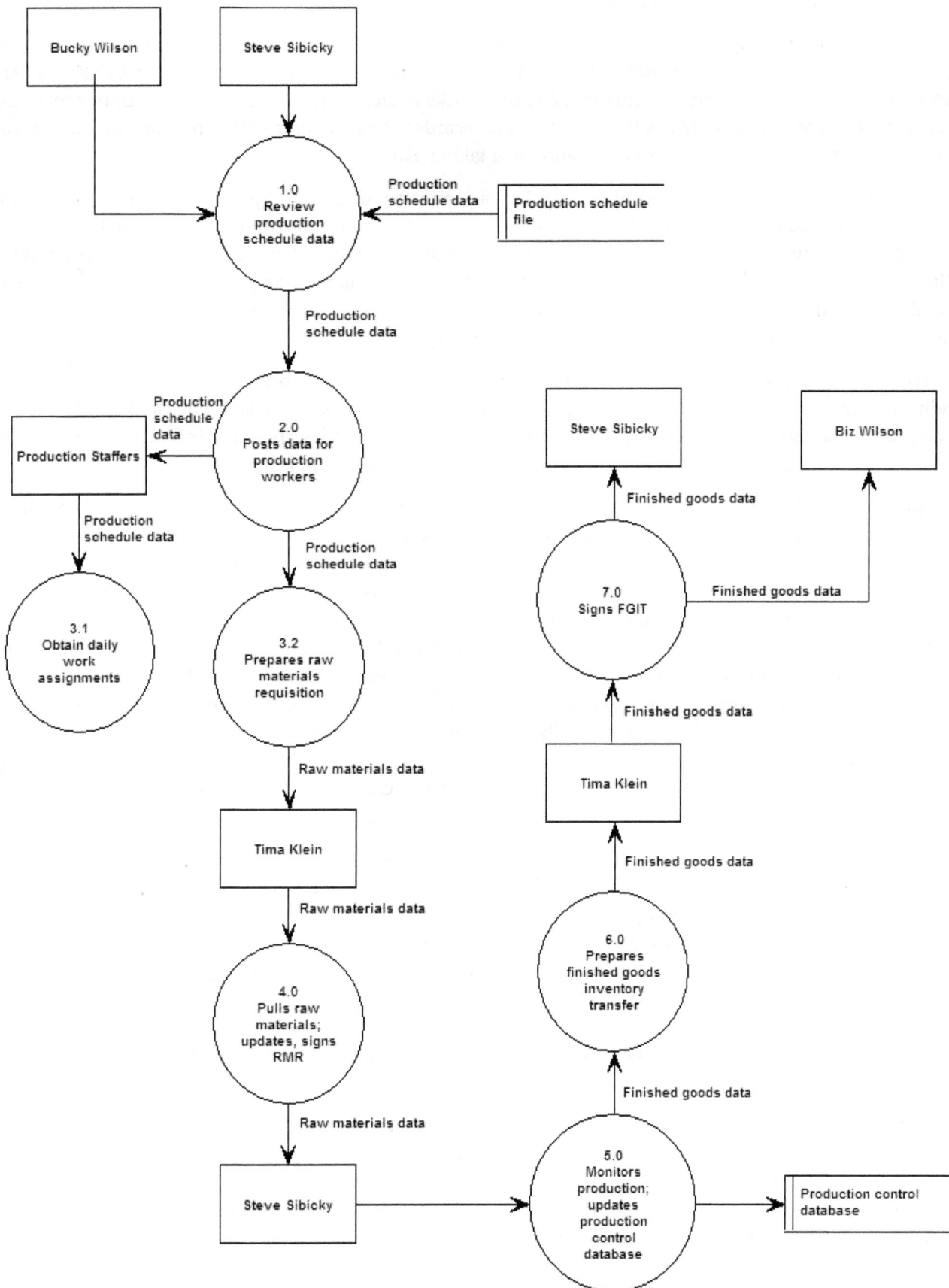

Chapter Core Question 4: What are the potential trouble points in internal control for the production control subprocess?

Internal Control Threats in the Production Control Subprocess

Spend a little more time examining Exhibit 8.2. What are the risks to Wolf River's production control subprocess? What internal controls would you put in place to reduce these risks? Consider our ASSRAV internal control toolkit as you evaluate the situation. Are there risks related to authorization? Insufficient supervision? A lack of segregation of duties? Are there appropriate records and documents for the transactions? Is there easy access to assets? Do you wish more verification was taking place?

Authorization: Production manager Steve Sibicky could misuse his approval powers and create fictitious raw materials requisitions to divert hardwoods pulled from the warehouse for personal use. Actually, it would be incredibly obvious from the standpoint of the production staffers if they observed timber being removed from the warehouse and loaded into Sibicky's pickup truck or set aside and not brought to the factory floor! In effect, production staffers' awareness of what ought to be coming from the warehouse (production schedule) serves as a source of supervision over the raw materials inventory.

Supervision: Sibicky actively monitors production control conditions. When problems occur, he promptly makes adjustments to production schedules and communicates significant delays and situations to Bucky Wilson. The warehouse manager, Tima Klein, appears to have appropriate knowledge about the inflow and outflow of raw materials and finished goods inventory. Overall, Wolf River's supervision is appropriate.

Separation of duties: Responsibilities for recordkeeping, custody, and approval are allocated between the production manager and warehouse manager. One person is not in control of all three tasks. This division of labor enhances internal control at Wolf River Hardwoods. Of course, there is a risk if Klein and Sibicky are colluding to steal raw materials from their employer. The presence of other staffers, however, acts as a control. Warehouse and factory staffers know when timber and finished goods are supposed to move through the production process. Can Sibicky alter or remove an entire customer job from the production schedule to cover their fraudulent activities? He has access to the production schedule file and production control database, so it's possible. Consider the challenges of covering up a scheme like this: Bucky Wilson and the production staffers would certainly notice a decrease in activity on the factory floor if raw materials were not in the warehouse; Biz Wilson would suspect something when he receives vendor invoices but fails to have corresponding production data for which raw materials are billed to customers; customers would wonder where their finished goods were if no timber was being converted into flooring, paneling, decorative beams, or custom-cut boards.

Records and documentation: Steve Sibicky frequently updates the production control database to reflect what's happening on the factory floor. Material requisition forms and finished goods inventory transfer forms provide evidence of the movement of physical goods through the production process. These documents contain the data to bill customers for work performed. Is it possible for fictitious records and documents to be created by Sibicky and Klein to conceal their errors or fraudulent behavior? Nothing's impossible. However, you are encouraged to reread the previous paragraph. Too many staffers are affected by the physical flow of inventory and rely on data from the production schedule and production control database. Questions about a lack of inventory, idle time, or discrepancies between vendor invoices and Wolf River's data would raise caution flags for the staffers and owner Bucky Wilson.

Access to assets: With control over the raw materials and finished goods inventories, warehouse manager Tima Klein is in a position of trust and responsibility. She needs to safeguard inventory movement in and out of the facility. Our vignette does not identify how many warehouse workers there are or if security cameras or locked storage areas are used. It is more likely for finished goods inventories to be stolen than the raw materials since unprocessed timber could weigh a ton or more and exceed 18 feet in length. The weight and size of finished flooring, paneling, and other custom-made items makes it easier to disappear from the warehouse. Additionally, no mention is made about segregating finished goods according to customer. A risk is present where items for different customer orders could be mixed together. This can complicate picking, packing, and delivery tasks (sales business process). Keeping different categories of inventory in distinct areas of the warehouse, making sure the warehouse is locked after work hours, and installing security cameras at warehouse doors are three internal controls to consider implementing.

> **ASSRAV**
> Authorization
> Supervision
> Segregation of duties
> Records & documentation
> Asset access restrictions
> Verification

Verification: Independent verification takes place at two points in the production control subprocess. Each day, Bucky Wilson reviews upcoming production schedules and is consulted by Steve Sibicky when significant production problems arise. Biz Wilson reconciles production data with vendor invoice data and customer sales orders. Neither are involved with warehouse and factory work and provide an objective perspective on the activities. With the small size of Wolf River Hardwoods, adequate verification is integrated into the production and manufacturing business process.

Before we wrap up this chapter, let's reflect on the production control subprocess vignette on pages 99 and 100. Not everything described in the narrative is documented in the physical data flow diagram shown in Exhibit 8.2. What is left out? Yes, the situation involving the equipment malfunction is not drawn in the flowchart. Why? The periodic call for repairs and maintenance can be omitted from the flowchart because it is not one of the daily, repetitive tasks occurring in the production control subprocess. Flowcharts depict the normal, routine functioning of something. We can't always imagine what could go wrong and incorporate it into a DFD.

But let's not ignore the possible internal control weaknesses related to maintenance and repair tasks. What are the internal control hot spots with the Wolf River PP&E repairs and maintenance activity? Do you get inspiration from what you learned in Chapter 7? STOP. Talk about them with your partner. Make a list in the tabular format commonly used in previous chapters. Remember to identify the internal control you'd put in place to deter or detect the internal control problem. Look over the table below only when you've finished preparing your table.

Internal Control Weakness	Internal Control Suggestion
Needed maintenance not performed according to schedule, causing delays in meeting customer delivery dates	Production manager Sibicky periodically reviews preventive maintenance and on-demand logs to ensure repairs and maintenance are being performed (supervision, records and documentation)
To save money, repairs performed in-house instead of calling manufacturers' technicians; run risk of inappropriate repairs being made	For more substantial repairs, Steve Sibicky or Bucky Wilson decide if work should be done by Wolf River's maintenance technicians (authorization)
Abusing terms of manufacturer maintenance contracts, service calls made to manufacturers when Wolf River staffers could undertake repair work	Maintenance contract service calls are placed by Biz Wilson after consultation with Steve Sibicky or Bucky Wilson (authorization, separation of duties)

The focus of internal controls for repair and maintenance tasks aims to safeguard assets and achieve management goals and objectives. It's necessary to guard the ways cash is spent. It could be disbursed for needed machine repairs or wasted on corrective work. This could be for manufacturer maintenance to fix a staffer's unsuccessful attempt at machine repair or for more serious repairs on a machine when maintenance should have been performed earlier but wasn't.

Likewise, safeguarding assets means protecting machinery and equipment: making sure it is in good operating condition and ready for its intended use. It also meets the objectives of Wolf River's management team. Providing high quality products to its customers in a timely fashion is vital to Wolf River Hardwoods – and all businesses, for that matter.

Summarizing Chapter 8

The production & manufacturing business process can be thought of as the hub of a wheel. It sits at the center of a manufacturing entity. Other business processes (sales, supply chain, and fixed assets) are the spokes of the wheel, meeting and connecting at the hub. Using fictitious company Wolf River Hardwoods, we examined data flows and internal control topics for the production scheduling and production control subprocesses. Which tools from our ASSRAV toolkit help create a strong system of manufacturing internal controls? All six tools provide benefits: authorizations, supervision, a separation of duties, records and documentation, restricted access to assets, and verification.

We're quickly coming to the end of our accounting information systems studies. Chapter 9, the penultimate chapter, talks about data flows and internal controls in the operations business process. In Chapter 10, you'll take a look at the human resources business process.

Chapter Core Vocabulary

Finished goods inventory transfer form – a document on which the production manager writes the items and quantities of finished goods being transferred from the factory floor to the warehouse.

Made-to-order business model – a manufacturing method where the customer specifies its product needs to the manufacturer, who then creates the goods according to these criteria.

Production & manufacturing business process – a cluster of activities allowing an entity to manage its raw materials and convert these raw materials into finished goods for sale to customers.

Raw materials requisition form – a document on which the production manager requests raw materials to be removed from the warehouse and brought to the factory floor for the day's production.

Read It, Do It – Mountaineer Electronics

Objectives

To identify internal control weaknesses in a company's manufacturing business process.

To understand how encryption, electronic authorization and verification, and supervision can reduce internal control weaknesses.

Introduction

Mountaineer Electronics produces custom integrated circuits (ICs) for use in consumer electronic devices such as mobile phones and portable DVD players. The company, headquartered in West Virginia, has four production facilities in North America. Mountaineer uses a "pull" manufacturing philosophy: all of its production activities are driven by customer orders. The company's customers transmit orders using global EDI standards.

Because of their proprietary nature, IC designs, engineering data and correspondence related to product plans are sent over secure telecommunication networks between Mountaineer and its customers.

Internal audit assignment

Ray Weaver is Mountaineer's director of internal and IT audit. You are a Mountaineer senior auditor. Mountaineer Electronics is a finalist for a contract to supply Irdos, a major global mobile device manufacturer, with ICs for a new product line. Because Irdos follows the Six Sigma quality process, a team from Irdos is scheduled to visit Mountaineer's four North American plants next month to evaluate whether Mountaineer meets strict production and operations requirements. In preparation for the Irdos inspection visit, you are asked to travel to the Mountaineer plant in Minnesota and evaluate internal controls at that facility.

Technology controls

You arrive at the factory in Minnesota and are met by the plant's Vice President of Operations, Eve Lander. She introduces you to her staff, gives you a brief tour of the facility, and shows you to your work cubicle.

You begin by talking with the plant's IT coordinator. He tells you that orders transmitted by Mountaineer's customers are not encrypted since they do not contain private or secret information. While customers use unique user logins and passwords to transmit the orders, Mountaineer has no way to determine the validity or authenticity of the order. Orders received are directly input to an application that identifies the item, quantity, and required delivery date at the customer's site. The software determines the optimal production schedule, taking into account all necessary resources (*e.g.* labor, raw material inventories, manufacturing cell availability, production schedules). Once an order is scheduled, the relevant information is sent to the production database. The production manager and supervisors use this database to monitor and control daily operations.

Customers are not sent an electronic confirmation of their orders unless there is a conflict or problem in meeting the delivery date.

Production controls

Next, you meet with Bishnu Gautam, production manager. During your conversation with him you learn that the supervisors rarely look at the summary reports generated daily by the production information system. They trust the reports to be accurate since the data "comes from the computer". As a result, the production schedule sometimes needs to be manually adjusted for manufacturing cell downtime, parts shortages, or workforce changes that were not updated in the employee scheduling application. These changes are typically entered into the database by plant workers and supervisors. User IDs and passwords are necessary to gain access to the database. However, daily activity logs detailing the database changes are not regularly examined by production supervisors.

Required

Prepare a memo for Ray Weaver, Mountaineer's audit director, about the Minnesota factory's readiness to do business with Irdos. Your memo will identify the internal control strengths and weaknesses, and explain the necessary changes to remediate internal control problems.

Chapter 9

Operations business process: college admissions; and records & registration

Chapter Core Questions

1. How does data flow though the college admissions subprocess?

2. At what points is the college admissions subprocess susceptible to internal control weaknesses?

3. What are the typical data flows in the records & registration subprocess?

4. What are the internal control hot spots in the records & registration subprocess?

Introduction

Service sector entities don't have production and manufacturing business processes. Instead, their offices and departments collaborate to deliver intangibles such as legal advice, accounting expertise, education, entertainment, or consulting knowledge to their clientele. The **operations business process** includes a diverse cluster of subprocesses that allow the organization to provide core services (the primary source of revenues) to customers. In some organizations, the subprocesses that directly support the core services are also called *operations*.

This chapter examines two supporting operations at a fictitious college. Byrne College, a small residential private four-year college located in the Midwest, enrolls 2,300 students in 37 majors. The 389-acre campus sits atop a bluff overlooking the Zaleski River. Its quiet environment offers students ample opportunities for academic reflection and personal recreation. The business subprocesses discussed here are not the most significant ones at the college but are presented to offer a representative look at operations support in service organizations. Byrne's offices responsible for food service, book sales, records & registration, campus public safety, mail processing / delivery, physical plant, admissions, information technology, and the library – among others – will be familiar to most students. But it's not practical to examine all of them in a single chapter. Therefore, Byrne's college admissions and records & registration subprocesses have been selected to illustrate data flows and internal controls in the operations business process.

Chapter Core Question 1: How does data flow though the college admissions subprocess?

College Admissions Subprocess Data Flows

Byrne's Office of Admissions is preparing for its triennial program review. This review is required of all offices and academic departments at Byrne. Stefan Fahim, admissions director, is responsible for preparing the review report. He has delegated most of the work related to the evaluation of the office's internal control weaknesses to Angelica Kanni, the admission office's associate director.

Late on a Wednesday autumn afternoon, Stefan and Angelica meet for coffee at the café in the library. Angelica wants to share a draft of what she's assembled for the internal control segment of the report. After ordering their beverages, they sit down at a table by the window overlooking the Zaleski River.

"Looking over our activities for this program review," starts Angelica, "it's clear we need to make some changes to our internal controls, particularly over data privacy and security," she states. She prepared a data flow diagram to help Stefan and the report's readers quickly see the relationships of the office's activities. This is shown in Exhibit 9.1

Exhibit 9.1 – Byrne College's Admissions Subprocess DFD

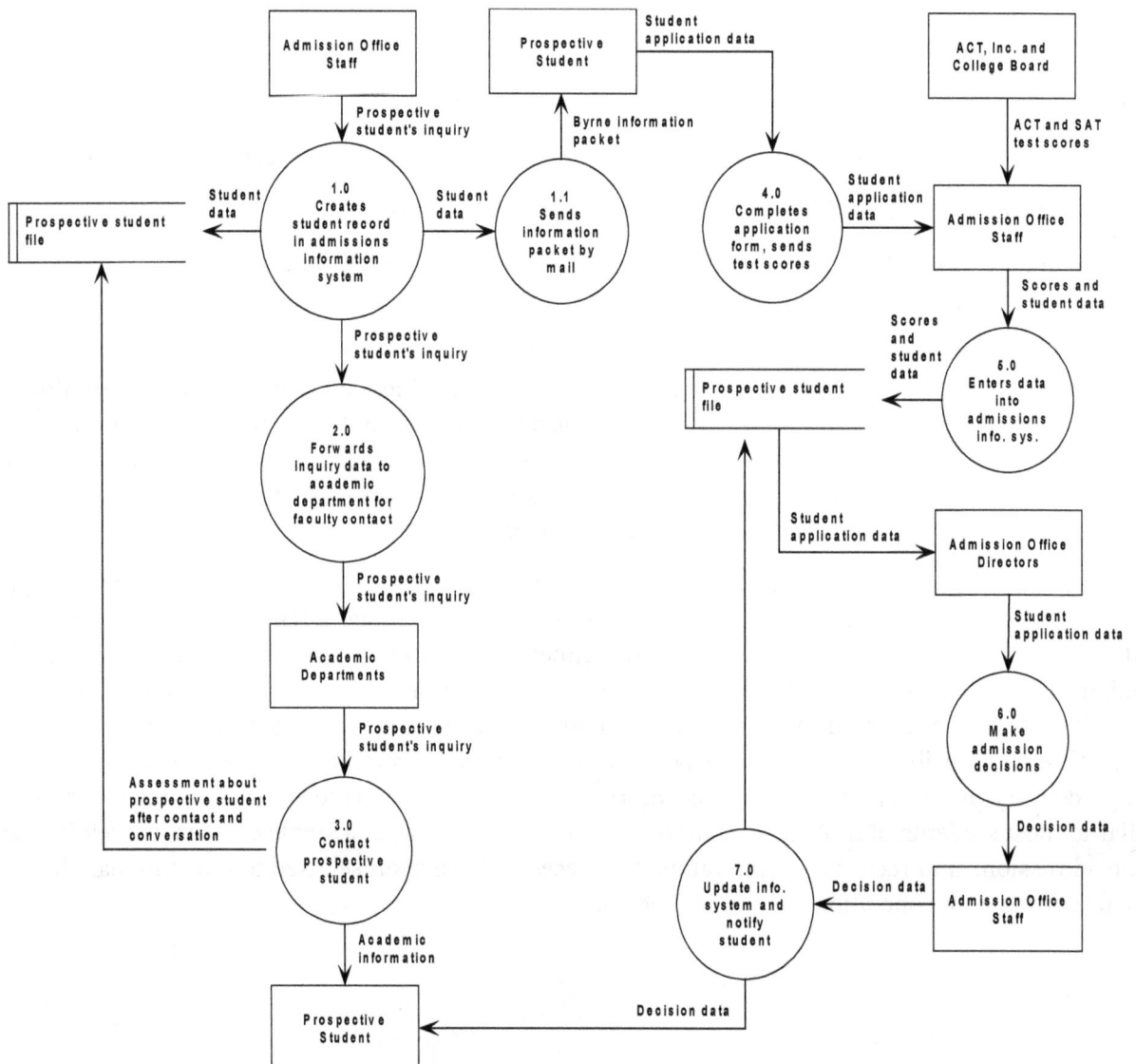

Based on the flowchart Angelica prepared, Stefan and Angelica think about the way the **admissions subprocess** is structured. It seems efficient and has met the college's needs in recent years. Both, however, wonder if Byrne should use its own online application. It's one of the modules included in the college's enterprise software. Or, they ponder, is it time to follow the lead of many colleges and adopt the Common Application[27]. On one hand, it would be advantageous for the Office of Admissions to have complete control over admissions data, but the benefits of using the online Common Application developed by the Common Application membership association seem to outweigh the loss of data control.

Stefan and Angelica are somewhat concerned about the access that Byrne faculty have to the prospective student file in the admissions information system. Faculty are encouraged to input their comments and feedback about the prospective students they speak with. But Angelica, in particular, isn't sure how much data in the files is accessible to faculty and if faculty can enter or edit data other than the contact comments.

Stefan expresses worries about the accuracy of the data entered into the admissions information system when Admissions Office staff transcribe information from hard copies of Byrne's application form and test scores reported from ACT, Inc. (ACT) and the College Board (SAT). Errors will be inevitable when the staff type data into the prospective student file. When the admission directors (Stefan, Angelica, and assistant director Craig Rozler) meet to make admission decisions, they have to consider the slim possibility that their admission decisions might be made in light of some inaccurate data from the prospective student file.

As Angelica and Stefan sip the last drops of their coffees, Stefan receives a text message from an admissions staffer. The conference call he's scheduled to have with someone from the Common Application membership committee starts in 15 minutes. "Time to head back to the office," he says as they grab their insulated drink mugs and walk to Padwin Hall.

What are the key activities in a small college's admissions subprocess? What must the Office of Admissions "get right" to ensure the admissions decision task is effective? STOP. Find a partner and jot down a list of activities you believe must be handled correctly and precisely by admissions office staffers. Don't read on until you've finished making your list.

Those activities central to accurate data gathering and decision making might include the following:

a. Initially inputting correct names, addresses (postal and e-mail), phone numbers, and academic interest areas for prospective students.

b. Clearly articulating the kind of information sought by admissions directors so faculty can add useful details from their phone conversations with prospective students, but restricting faculty access to student details.

c. Accurately entering prospective students' application data and ACT/SAT test scores into the admission information system.

d. Correctly updating the prospective students file for admission decisions.

Why are these activities material to the admissions decision? If student names, contact details, or academic interest areas contain mistakes the remaining tasks become cumbersome (trying to phone or send an e-mail message) and may result in lost contact with the prospective students. Inappropriate information packets could be sent to students (*e.g.* the psychology information packet is mailed to a student interested in biology) and faculty from the wrong department might contact the prospective student. It's an embarrassment – not to

---

27   The Common Application for Undergraduate College Admission. Available at: https://www.commonapp.org/CommonApp/Default.aspx

mention the incompetence communicated – when the college doesn't connect the proper department's professors with the student.

Once prospective students submit their applications, Office of Admissions staffers must accurately update student records; test scores received from ACT, Inc. and the College Board need to be correctly entered into students' records. These source documents provide the key input to the admissions directors' decisions. Once Stefan, Angelica, and Craig make their admission choices, decisions need to be correctly communicated to the students. None of these directors wants to be responsible for retracting a student's admission offer because of a mistake made when data was entered into the admission information system!

Chapter Core Question 2: At what points is the college admissions subprocess susceptible to internal control weaknesses?

Internal Control Weaknesses in the College Admissions Subprocess

Back at Padwin Hall, Angelica examines the notes from her meeting with Stefan. She knows that the present series of activities in the Office of Admissions has several internal control weak spots but is unsure about what to do to address these weaknesses.

Reflect on the four key activities identified in the previous section. What's the potential threat or risk each poses to the admissions subprocess?

a. *Initially inputting correct names, addresses (postal and e-mail), phone numbers, and academic interest areas for prospective students.* When Byrne's records and documents are inaccurate, mistakes will affect anyone accessing the data.

b. *Clearly articulating the kind of information sought by admissions directors so faculty can add useful details from their phone conversations with prospective students, but restricting faculty access to student details.* Faculty involvement doesn't pose a threat to the admissions decision making process itself. In fact, Byrne's practice of having professors contact prospective students and submit feedback about their conversations adds an interesting dimension to the admissions evaluation. The risk of such faculty access, however, is how data contained in the prospective student file could be misused by faculty.

c. *Accurately entering prospective students' application data and ACT/SAT test scores into the admission information system.* Prospective students with similar names might have the wrong data entered into their records. Test score data could be mistyped, under- or overstating student performance on those entrance examinations. Admission decisions might be erroneous because of these data entry mistakes.

d. *Correctly updating the prospective students file for admission decisions.* Incorrectly entered admission decisions that are communicated to prospective students' causes embarrassment and sends a message that the Office of Admissions and Byrne College isn't careful or doesn't pay attention to details.

Next, create a table that presents your recommendations for strengthening the internal control weaknesses for these key activities. Remember to rely on our ASSRAV toolkit as a starting point for your internal controls. Please organize the table as follows:

Internal Control Weakness	Recommended Internal Control	ASSRAV Tool Utilized

Only after you've finished preparing your table should you continue reading.

Here are a few suggestions for the internal controls that the Office of Admissions might implement to enhance the security and accuracy of prospective student file data.

Internal Control Weakness	Recommended Internal Control	ASSRAV Tool Utilized
Data entry mistakes (initial)	Ask staffers to review data input for accuracy	None
Faculty misuse of student data	Limit faculty activity to read-only (name, phone number, academic interests)	Asset access restrictions
Data entry mistakes with subsequent updates to student records	Admissions directors examine list of accepted students before notifying these students	Verification

None of our ASSRAV tools really fit the first suggested internal control, self-review of data input. To segregate duties where two or more staffers enter the data or review the data entered by another staffer is to introduce unnecessary complexity to the data entry task. Nor is it useful to have an admissions office supervisor monitor or look over the work performed by office staffers. The best control we can hope for is to have staffers doing data entry to carefully look over their work to make sure that student names, phone numbers, postal and e-mail addresses, application form data, and examination scores have properly been keyed into the records.

Remember our primary constraint related to internal controls: the cost to implement the control should be less than the benefit derived from the control. To require several staffers to review the work of others or ask supervisors to examine data input for correctness violates this cost-benefit rule. If nothing else, it slows down the office activities and takes supervisors away from more significant work they perform. And all for the sake of ensuring proper data entry? No, Byrne College's admissions office can simply raise its expectation of the quality of work its staffers perform and encourage everyone to double-check data input to the admissions information system before pressing the "enter" or "submit" key.

Misuse or abuse of data by anyone with legitimate access is a constant source of worry in any organization. At Byrne, it doesn't only come from the faculty adding their comments to the prospective students' records. For instance, Office of Admissions, Financial Aid Office, Records Office, and Information Technology Office staffers have clearance to access student data. To illustrate how those with permission to retrieve, create, and use data pose a threat to internal control, we'll examine the faculty's ability to read and update data in the prospective student file.

One tool to limit the amount and type of data to which the faculty have access is to restrict viewing to essential data. These would include the student's name, phone number, and areas of academic interest. Once the professors make their admissions phone contacts and want to add comments to the records, a blank data entry form or website that imports the comments into the records should be used, further limiting the access faculty have to student data. Additionally, Byrne College needs to rely on the integrity of faculty and non-teaching staff to respect the trusted positions they hold – and the confidentiality of the data available to them in their daily work – and not misuse this trust for personal gain.

Lastly, there's the problem of inaccurate data making its way into the prospective students' records and its use to admit or deny admission to students. How can Byrne's admissions team be sure the list of admitted students is accurate before admissions letters are sent to students? Although admissions staffers try to be attentive to data input, there will be the periodic error entering an ACT or SAT score, scanning and adding a reference letter, or updating other student data.

One control that can be implemented is for one or more of the admissions directors to review the admitted students list and reconcile the acceptance and rejection decisions with the student data one last time before releasing decision letters. Such verification might help the college avoid the embarrassment of sending a rejection letter to a student that should have been admitted or an acceptance letter to someone who had been turned down for admission. Of course, care in initially handling and entering data is the best internal control but errors are unavoidable. The directors' final verification is the last opportunity to ensure accuracy in Byrne College's admission process.

Regardless of the office or task in which it occurs, ensuring integrity and security is a key element in the effort to safeguard intangible (data) assets. All internal control systems need tools, policies, and – most challenging to implement – staffer behaviors and attitudes that promote data protection.

Chapter Core Question 3: What are the typical data flows in the records & registration subprocess?

Data Flows in the Records & Registration Subprocess

The **records & registration subprocess** provides critical support to faculty, students, and non-teaching staff. It is the central data collection point for student grades, source of information about students' progress toward graduation requirements, distributor of unofficial and official academic transcripts, and coordinator of semester course schedules. Many might agree with the statement that the records & registration subprocess is the most critical academic support operation at institutions of higher education.

Paula Frezatti is Byrne College's Records Office director. She supervises a staff of three fulltime workers and four work-study students. One of her fulltime staffers is retiring two months from now; Paula decides to use the occasion of hiring a new person as a perfect time to develop a physical data flow diagram depicting tasks in the Records Office. She knows it will be useful for the new staffer to have a flowchart to identify some of the office's major activities. Likewise, the exercise offers Paula and her staff an opportunity to evaluate the environment for internal control weak spots and to create and implement controls that will foster stronger data security and integrity. You'll recall that this was an important control objective in Byrne's Office of Admissions as well.

Exhibit 9.2 – Byrne College's Records Subprocess DFD

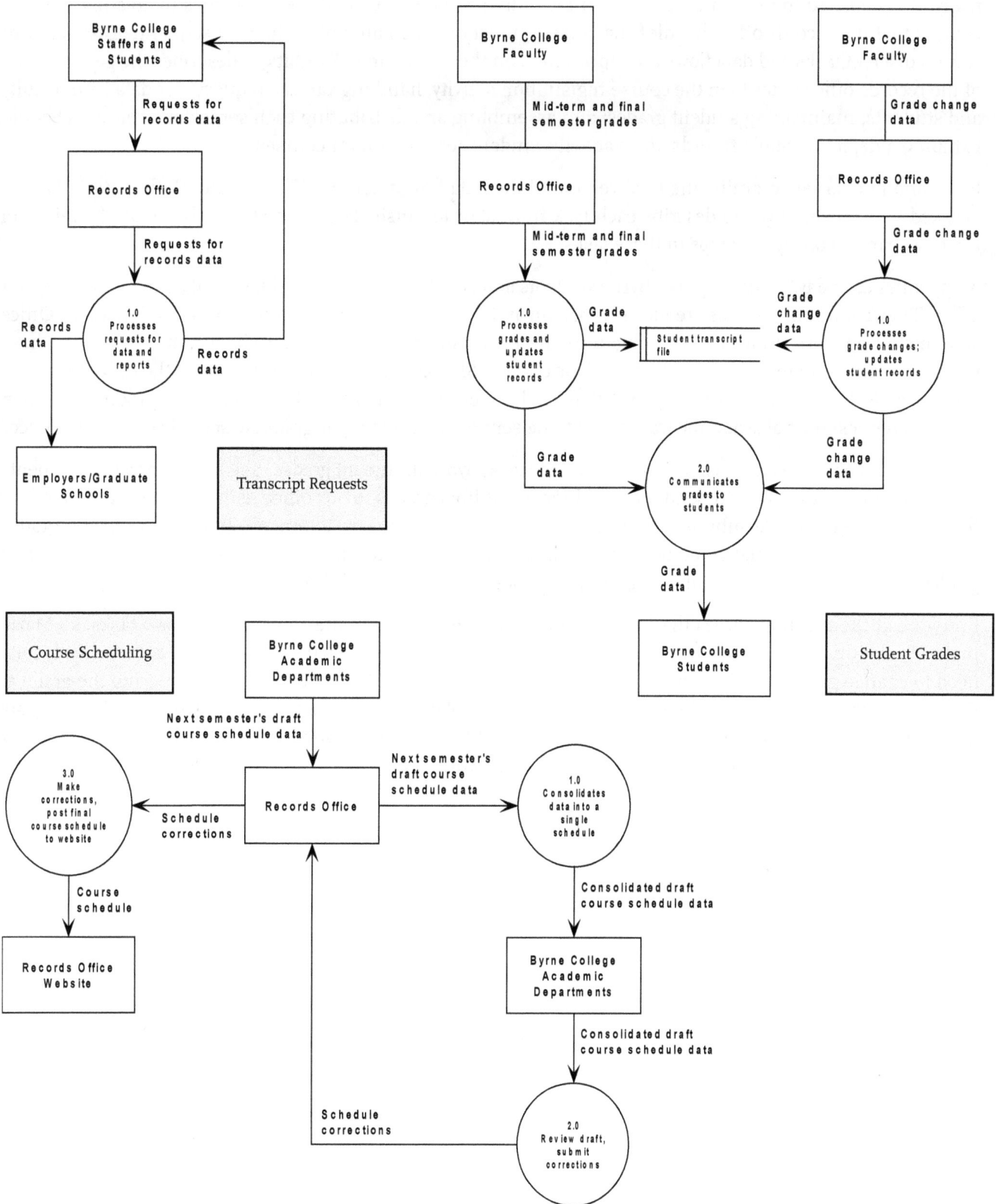

Paula meets with her three fulltime staffers one afternoon to create the first draft of the data flow diagram. Over several days the staffers add their comments and make modifications. In a week's time, the flowchart is ready. It is depicted in two parts, reflected in Exhibits 9.2 and 9.3. One of the challenges in creating the flowchart is that the records office handles many tasks, most of which are not performed sequentially. Therefore, several discreet tasks and data flows are represented on these diagrams. Exhibit 9.2 describes the general work of the records office other than the course registration activity: handling various requests for data from faculty and students; maintaining student grades; and assembling and distributing each semester's course schedule. Exhibit 9.3 depicts a single records office activity, student registration for courses.

Paula and her staffers examine the final version of the data flow diagrams. The retiring staffer, Marie Parnas, is asked to use Exhibit 9.2 to describe each task from start to finish. The other staffers listen as she relies on the flowchart to convey the steps in these tasks.

"Many times each day," Marie begins, "Byrne students and staff have needs for all kinds of data maintained by our office. They communicate those requests in person at the Records Office or via phone or e-mail. Records Office staff, including work study students, obtain the necessary information and share it with the requestor. These responses can be shared in person, by e-mail, or phone." She pauses. Raul Saavedra, one of the office's fulltime staffers, adds, "and generally the only time that hard copies of documents and information is produced is when students request official academic transcripts to be sent to an employer or graduate school admissions office."

Marie focuses on the second task with which the office is involved: student grades. She thinks for a few moments then starts to explain. "Faculty send their mid-term and final grades to our office using the website created for this step. Once the grade submission deadline passes, we use software to process students' semester grades and update their individual grade records in our transcript file. After this, we mail paper copies of mid-term grades to students' campus mailboxes and final semester grades to their home addresses."

Everyone at the meeting agrees that the flowchart accurately portrays the steps in these two tasks, so Marie moves to the third task shown in Exhibit 9.2, grade changes made by faculty. She starts, "sometimes faculty need to change grades that have been assigned to students. Maybe they made a mistake entering the grade at the website or calculating it in their gradebook," Marie explains. Raul adds another explanation. He suggests that a grade of incomplete might have been assigned at the end of the previous semester because of the student's serious illness that didn't allow him to finish the work in a course.

Exhibit 9.3 – Byrne College's Registration Subprocess DFD

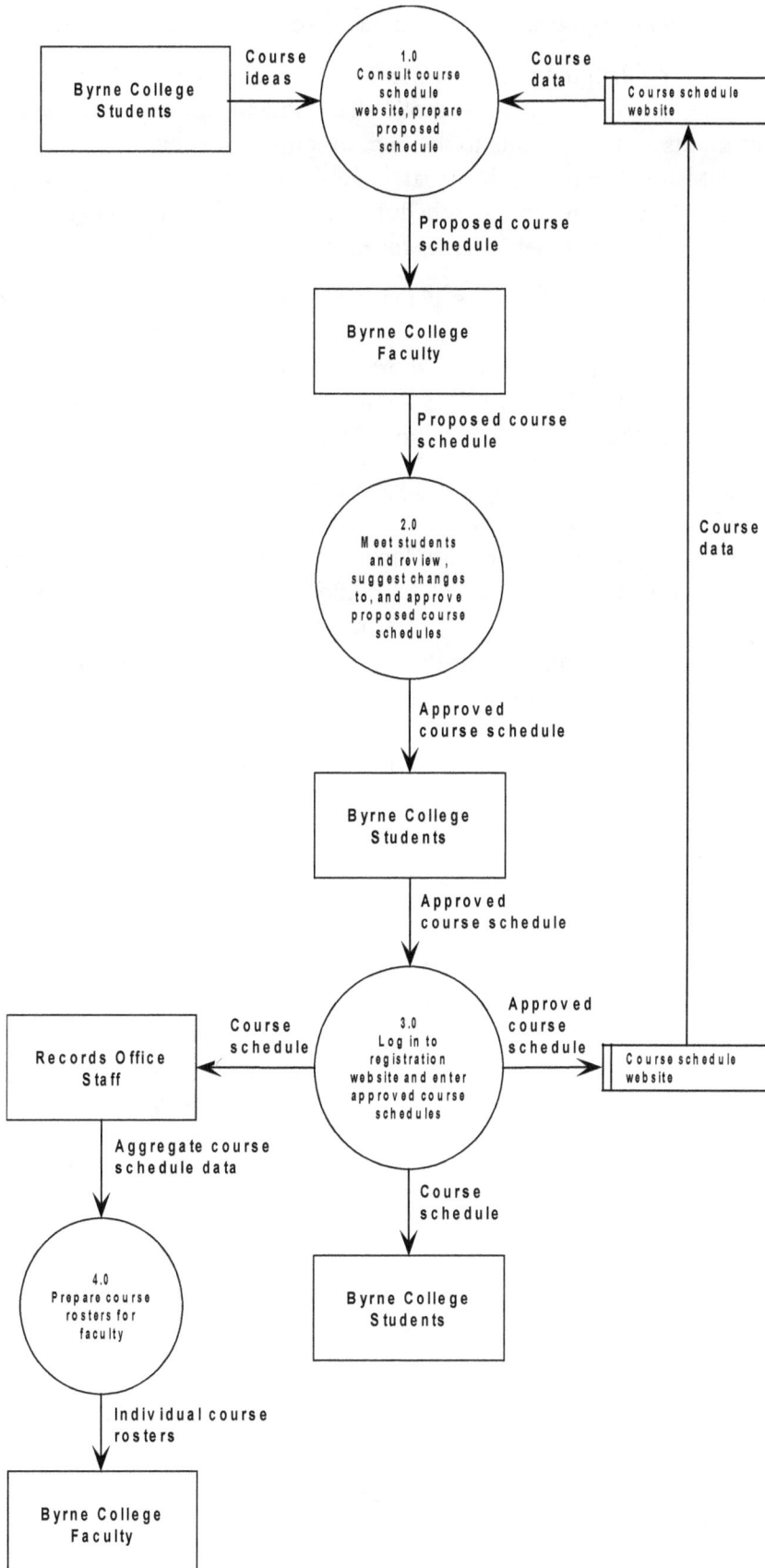

"After a student completes the outstanding assignments or examinations," he says, "the professor needs to change the incomplete grade to the correct grade." All shake their heads in agreement; Marie proceeds to describe the final task shown on the data flow diagram, assembling and distributing semester course schedules.

"About one month before we publish the next semester's course schedule, academic departments send their draft schedules to our office," Marie states. "We compile all of the schedule data into a single draft schedule for all courses in all departments and return this to the departments for review. There are always corrections to be made, so these are sent back to our office by department secretaries. After we get all of the corrections we prepare the final version of the semester course schedule. Then we upload the schedule to the Records Office website for students to use in selecting their courses for next semester."

Again, everyone nods in agreement that Marie's explanation of the process as shown on the data flow diagram matches what actually happens in the office. Paula suggests they take a short break from the review to grab tea and coffee and snacks. After all, time's running short to enjoy Marie's homemade cream puffs. Once she's retired she won't be bringing them to the office. "Yes I will," insists Marie, "but maybe not as often as I do now." Raul, Paula, and Alexa Navalny, the office's other fulltime staffer, smile.

While sipping coffee and eating cream puffs, Paula suggests that Alexa describe the course registration activity depicted in Exhibit 9.3. She reaches for the data flow diagram, studies it for a minute, and begins her explanation of the tasks as reflected in the flowchart. "Students have ideas about the courses they want to take next semester. They consult the course schedule located on the Records Office website and put together a tentative course schedule. When they meet with their faculty advisors to discuss their proposed schedules, their advisors review, make recommendations for changes, then approve students' schedules. Later on, during the designated time to register for classes, students enter their course schedules at the Records Office website. Each time a student schedule is entered software updates the number of seats available in a course and uploads this current capacity data to the course schedule on the Records Office website."

Raul jumps in and reminds, "this is necessary so that students don't develop tentative schedules based on courses that are already filled."

"Right," says Paula.

Alexa finishes her explanation. "Paper copies of the schedules are sent to students' campus mailboxes after students enter their schedules at the website. At the conclusion of the student registration period, the Records Office reviews the course data and compiles class rosters to distribute to the faculty the day before the semester starts."

Paula and the others are satisfied that their data flow diagrams accurately represent what happens in the office. The time spent earlier – reviewing and editing the flowcharts – certainly paid off.

Chapter Core Question 4: What are the internal control hot spots in the records & registration subprocess?

Records & Registration Subprocess Internal Control Weaknesses

Given the sensitive nature of the data maintained by and available to Records Office staffers, this subprocess at Byrne College deserves special attention. You've read accounts of the office's key activities in the previous section. Now you will consider internal control weaknesses inherent in this subprocess and develop a cluster of controls aimed at deterring/discouraging and detecting these threats.

STOP. Find a partner with whom you can study Exhibits 9.2 and 9.3 and review Marie's descriptions of the activities depicted in those flowcharts. Please make a list of internal control risks to which these activities are susceptible. Think about the nature of the data, the people providing and using the data, and the methods by which the data moves in and out of the office. Do not continue reading until your partner and you have completed your list.

What follows is not an exhaustive list of the subprocess' vulnerabilities; your collection of risks will certainly include items not enumerated here.

Handling requests for data

1. Because student records data is protected by federal law (the Family Educational Rights and Privacy Act[28]) it is essential to verify the identity of the person requesting data and determine whether the requestor is entitled to receive the data. One internal control risk is sharing student records data with unauthorized persons.

2. Another risk is related to the methods used to communicate student records data. Telephone and e-mail, in particular, pose a potential internal control problem since it isn't easy to confirm that the caller or sender of the message is, in fact, the student or Byrne College staffer the person claims to be.

3. Work study students employed by the Records Office have access to all student record data and might compromise data privacy.

Submitting student grades and changing student grades

4. When entering mid-term or final semester grades – or updating grades from a previous semester – faculty might input the wrong grade at the grade submission website.

5. Records Office software might incorrectly process student grades, resulting in inaccurate student semester grade reports and academic transcripts.

Assembling and distributing each semester's course schedule

6. Records Office staffers make mistakes in compiling/consolidating each department's schedules into the master course schedule.

7. Academic departments don't catch all mistakes when they review the consolidated draft course schedule prepared by the Records Office.

8. Records Office doesn't update master course schedule for all revisions made by the academic department secretaries.

9. Wrong version of the final course schedule is uploaded to the Records Office website.

Course registration

10. Students make mistakes inputting course data at the registration website.

11. Registration software fails to update course schedule website after each student completes registration.

These internal control vulnerabilities originate from several root sources: authentication of users; failure to carefully review data; and software processing errors. When you consider these causes you can develop effective controls for the Records Office to implement. With your partner, identify internal controls you'd suggest for the 11 weaknesses noted above. Please organize your response according to the table format we've commonly used in this textbook. Don't forget to link the control to one of the ASSRAV tools.

---

28   Family Educational Rights and Privacy Act. U.S. Department of Education. Available at: http://www.ed.gov/policy/gen/guid/fpco/ferpa/index.html

Internal Control Weakness	Recommended Internal Control	ASSRAV Tool Utilized

Once you are you are done with your task you may conclude the chapter's reading. Does your table have suggestions such as the ones identified below?

Internal Control Weakness	Recommended Internal Control	ASSRAV Tool Utilized
Sharing student records data with unauthorized persons	Release data only to student or Byrne College staff/faculty advisor; to parent or guardian only if student has signed FERPA waiver	Authorization, records & documentation
Records Office staffer failure to confirm identity of requestor	Require student inquiries to be made in person and substantiated by showing Byrne ID card; e-mail and phone inquiries only for staff and faculty	Records & documentation
Work study students' access to student record data	Restrict types of tasks performed and records to be accessed by student workers (ID/password restrictions)	Authorization, asset access restrictions
Faculty input wrong grades at website	Website prominently displays reminder for faculty to review grades before submitting	N/A – see discussion about self-review of input on page 111
Records Office software incorrectly processes student grades	Before each mid-term and final grade reporting period, IT department runs test transactions to verify correct processing	Verification
Records Office staffers make mistakes in consolidating draft master course schedule	Records Office director periodically reviews consolidated draft schedule	Verification
Academic departments fail to correct errors/omissions in consolidated draft schedule	Academic secretaries and faculty carefully review/update course data before submitting to records office	N/A – see discussion about self-review of input on page 111

Records Office staffers neglect to update master course schedule for departmental revisions	Assign one Records Office staffer to handle updates from academic departments, director reviews final version before uploading to website	Separation of duties, verification
Upload wrong version of final course schedule	Records Office staffer responsible for task double-checks that correct file is uploaded	N/A – see discussion about self-review of input on page 111
Students enter wrong data during course registration	Website prominently displays reminder for students to review data before submitting	N/A – see discussion about self-review of input on page 111
Registration module fails to update course schedule	Before each registration period, IT department runs test transactions to verify correct processing	Verification

Recapping the Operations Business Process

In Chapter 4 we introduced the operations business process as comprising those subprocesses in support of the organization's core sales and supply chain business processes. Retailing and manufacturing entities rely on a number of departments to sustain their sales and production/manufacturing processes. Discussions of information technology, physical plant services, public relations, and customer service activities were presented as illustrations. Many more such supporting activities exist, such as the legal office, food service, mailroom, and security areas.

In this chapter we made an in-depth study of the operations business process from the perspective of an organization in the service sector: a college. Since there are no production and manufacturing business processes in a service entity we can use the term *operations* to refer to two aspects of the entity. We may call the offices that provide the primary revenue-generating processes as operations. At fictitious Byrne College these would be the academic departments. Yet we can also denote the collection of subprocesses helping the organization to provide these key services as operations, such as the athletic offices, academic resource center, career services, health center, and as exemplified in detail in Chapter 9, the admissions and records offices.

Remember that the term *operations* can represent a number of areas in an organization depending on how that organization views the concept of *operations*. What have been presented in this textbook as examples of operations is but a representative sample of supporting activities and offices. Consider a hospital, bank, hotel, transportation company, government agency, or not-for-profit social service organization (such as the Osborne Senior Center from Chapter 4). What constitutes their activities that reinforce the core service/revenue-providing processes will be as unique as the organizations themselves. Here, the objective is to acquaint you with these supporting business processes and raise your awareness of their internal control risks.

As we wrap up our introduction to accounting information systems, business processes, and internal controls, Chapter 10 takes us into the human resources business process. Ready to tackle the final chapter?

Chapter Core Vocabulary

Admissions subprocess – a cluster of related activities performed to recruit, evaluate, and admit students to a college.

Operations business process – the collection of activities that allow a service entity to provide core services (revenue generating services) to its clientele and the subprocesses directly supporting these core services.

Records & registration subprocess – a group of tasks conducted to provide the central data collection point for student grades, serve as the source of information about students' progress toward graduation requirements, distribute unofficial and official academic transcripts, and coordinate semester course schedules.

Read It, Do It – White Grass Savings Bank

Objectives

To recognize internal control weaknesses in a bank's operations business process and make recommendations to strengthen them.

To understand how subcontracting services to a vendor complicates a system of internal control.

Introduction

You are a fulltime college student majoring in accounting. The professor of your auditing class has given your classmates and you two weeks to complete the following experiential assignment related to your chapter on operational auditing.

Select a local organization and learn about one of its operations business processes. Meet with the organization's chief financial officer, controller, accountant, or business manager. Make sure the person you choose is able to talk to you in detail about operations. After understanding the process, think about the internal controls used in the process. On April 4, each team will make a brief oral presentation about what it learned. Your presentation should include a data flow diagram of the process. Teams will identify the organization's internal control strengths and weaknesses, and recommend controls to reduce or limit the weaknesses. You will work in teams of three on this assignment.

The Experience

You team up with Ernie Jensen and Nadia Messier on the assignment. The three of you choose to examine the internal controls over ATM activities at a local bank, White Grass Savings Bank, since Ernie's sister is the chief financial officer. You contact Beverly Jensen and set up a meeting to visit the bank and learn about its controls.

On the day of the meeting Beverly shows your team around the bank, and then takes you across the street to the building where the bank's drive-thru lanes and the ATM are located (shown on page 121, left). Beverly unlocks the door that leads to the small room where the ATM is situated. The machine, about four feet tall and three feet wide, is divided into two sections (shown on page 121, right). The top section of the machine contains the receipt printer, the keypad and LCD screen that customers use in transacting their business, and a small video camera. To access all of these components, you need to have a key to the lid covering the top section of the ATM.

Beverly explains that the bottom section of the ATM is accessible by a dual-lock system: a key and a combination. Inside are two cassettes that contain the currency. Twenty dollar bills are stacked in one cassette; five dollar bills are placed in the other.

After the tour, all of you return to the main bank building and sit in a small conference room to talk about the bank's internal controls for the ATM. Ernie asks how cash in the ATM is replenished. Beverly says that one employee, typically the head teller of the drive-thru bank, has the key to the ATM room and the keys and the combination to the ATM. At the start and conclusion of each day she checks the quantity of $20 and $5 bills in the ATM, and if low, takes money from a cash drawer in the drive-thru teller line and adds it to the ATM cassettes. If the head teller is not available to do this, one of the other tellers from the drive-thru bank handles the replenishment task. Also at the end of the day the head teller balances the cash balance for the ATM. Of course, the total amount of cash in the ATM at day's end should equal the beginning balance plus transfers of cash from the teller line and customer cash deposits, less customer cash withdrawals.

Nadia is curious how White Grass handles ATM repairs. Beverly explains that the bank does not perform any maintenance. Instead, it has a contract for repair services with the ATM manufacturer. The contact specifies that the company will send a service technician to the bank during regular business hours and can provide after-hours repairs for an additional cost. White Grass Savings Bank's management feels it is imperative to repair the ATM within six hours after a problem is first identified, even if that means paying the additional fee for the technician to fix the machine at night or on weekends. When the ATM malfunctions, the machine automatically sends a request for service to the manufacturer. You ask whether a bank employee meets the technician at the bank to let the technician into the drive-thru office for after-hours and weekend repairs. Beverly responds that the manufacturer's technicians have keys to the drive-thru facility and know the security code to disarm the alarm system, and therefore it's unnecessary for a bank employee to show up. The technicians take care of everything, including arming the security system and locking up the drive-thru bank office when they leave.

Ernie, Nadia, and you thank Beverly Jensen for her time and the information, and then return to campus. Based on what you've learned from Beverly, you agree to prepare a draft of the section about the strengths and weaknesses related to the ATM operations. You'll meet with Ernie and Nadia tomorrow evening at HK Donuts to review the assignment and show them the draft of your portion of the project.

Required

Prepare, using PowerPoint, your portion of the assignment. Remember, you are handling the strengths and weaknesses of White Grass Savings Bank's ATM operations.

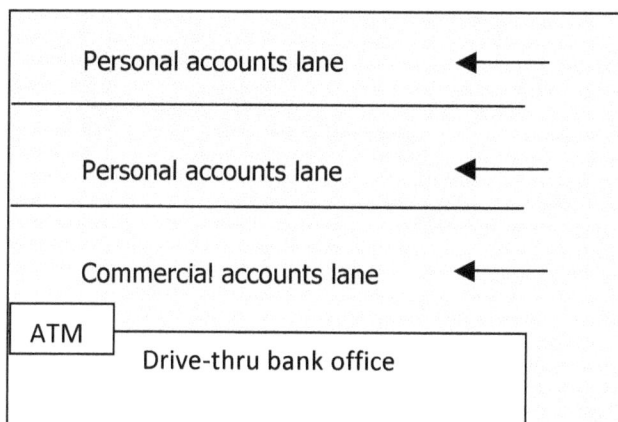

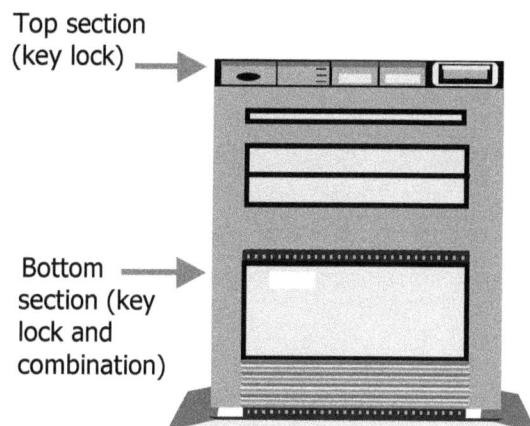

Chapter 10

Human resources business process: recruitment/hiring; and payroll

Chapter Core Questions

1. What are the common data flows and internal control weaknesses in the recruitment/hiring subprocess?

2. How does data move through the payroll subprocess?

3. What are possible internal control trouble points in the payroll subprocess?

Introduction

The **human resources business process** encompasses a broad collection of subprocesses including recruitment/ hiring, career development, training, payroll, benefits administration, and government reporting. Generally performed by the human resources department or office, the specific activities undertaken will vary according to an entity's size, nature, degree of centralization, and organizational culture and tradition. It is not this text-book's purpose to cover internal controls for such a range of activities. Rather, you are introduced to two of the most fundamental areas in human resources: recruitment/hiring and payroll.

In many textbooks the payroll subprocess is commonly associated with the human resources business process despite the fact that the routine, repetitive tasks of timekeeping, processing payroll, and distributing net wages is the work of staffers in the accounting department. Some entities include the payroll clerks and managers as part of their HR staff, and in others, the accounting staff. The payroll subprocess, however, has a clear and important link to the human resources business process when it comes to authorizing staffers to be added to and removed from the payroll and approving wage increases and job description changes (promotions, demotions, or lateral job movements). For these key reasons, the payroll subprocess is included in this chapter – along with the recruiting/hiring subprocess – as representative activities of a typical human resources function.

Jackson Transportation is a regional ground transport company. Established by Lee Jackson in 1978, members of the extended Jackson family own 100 percent of the common stock of this closely held company. Jackson offers two types of services to its clients: moving furniture for individuals and businesses; and transporting objects requiring special handling and security, such as rare books and works of art, for museums, libraries, or individual collectors. Each service category places unique demands on Jackson's drivers to be quick, professional, and careful.

Jackson Transportation recently scored a managerial coup when it hired a new chief financial officer. Fiona Colgate formerly served as chief financial officer for a well-known national carrier. Colgate brings extensive industry experience and new perspectives that complement Lee Jackson's management style. Among the projects she wants to wrap up by the end of her first six months at Jackson is a review of all administrative business processes. Colgate chose the human resources business process as the first to evaluate.

Colgate teams up with Jackson's human resources director, Nathan Glendale, to understand daily human resources activities. Glendale suggests to Colgate that she have conversations with the key staffers in each area, Katy Hoogerland (recruiting/hiring) and Nicole Villars (payroll).

Chapter 10, using the Jackson Transportation scenario, discusses data flows and internal controls in two human resources subprocesses. Are you ready to investigate the transactions and essential internal controls? Let's hit the road.

Chapter Core Question 1: *What are the common data flows and internal control weaknesses in the recruitment/hiring subprocess?*

Data Flows in the Recruitment/Hiring Subprocess

Fiona Colgate and Katy Hoogerland meet for juice and coffee at 10:00am. It's a crisp autumn morning, and Fiona runs into the company café with her wool scarf tightly wrapped around her neck. "I'm not used to these cool fall days," says Colgate.

Hoogerland describes the company's recruiting/hiring activities to Colgate. Jackson hires experienced commercial truck drivers whose driving records are unblemished and have valid CDLs (commercial driving licenses) and appropriate endorsements. An a sign of his keen management style, Lee Jackson made the decision a few years ago to rely on the "temp-to-hire" approach for recruiting and hiring all staffers, from business office staff and dispatchers to diesel mechanics and parts technicians – even drivers. All staffers begin work as temporary hires, chosen and placed at Jackson Transportation by a national staffing agency specializing in the transportation and logistics sectors. After a six-month probation period, Jackson can choose to hire the temporary staffer. The temp-to-hire phenomenon is not unusual for a manufacturer, but Jackson Transportation ranks among the few ground transportation companies that have adopted this staffing strategy.

> A staffing contractor handles recruiting, interviewing, and hiring activities for its clients

Hoogerland tells Colgate she will outline the steps involved in the recruiting/hiring subprocess with an example of hiring a truck driver. Regardless of the type of hire, the activity is the same. "So if the business office needs an accounting clerk or the shop requires a parts technician or mechanic's helper, all requests for new hires follow these steps," says Hoogerland.

When Jackson needs to hire a driver, the manager of the unit requesting the hire sends a written detailed job description for the position to Hoogerland. She confirms the request with the appropriate vice-president (in this case, operations), then contacts the staffing vendor. The vendor reviews Jackson's job requirements and selects a short list of three candidates. Those candidates are interviewed by the staffing vendor and the one chosen for the assignment is instructed to contact Katy Hoogerland about the start date and location. In essence, the staffing vendor is the recruiter and handles advertising, screening, interviewing, and hiring. Jackson Transportation pays a fee to the staffing vendor for these services. If Jackson opts to hire the staffer after the six-month probation period, it can. This happens without paying additional fees to the vendor, a practice common among large companies using the services of staffing consultants.

If the staffer passes the six-month probation period and is hired by Jackson Transportation, Hoogerland works with the staffer to sign an employment contract (with standardized job titles and rates of salary) and complete the required tax and employee benefits forms. She does not perform an additional background or driving investigation since this would have been conducted six months earlier by the staffing vendor.

Every quarter, Hoogerland holds a half-day new staffer orientation for those hired in the previous quarter. The orientation covers company policies and practices and staffer benefits. A new component of orientation was added in the last few months: diversity training.

Fiona Colgate listens carefully as Katy Hoogerland explains what happens. Fiona takes detailed notes about these tasks, knowing she'll refer to them later on when she analyzes the entirety of human resources subprocesses.

Recruitment/Hiring Subprocess Internal Control Weaknesses

STOP. What internal control strengths and weaknesses are exhibited in Jackson Transportation's recruiting and hiring subprocess? Find a partner and prepare a list. Look at the table below only when you finished writing your list.

Internal Control Strengths	Internal Control Weaknesses
Uses staffing vendor for recruiting, tapping into broader pools of applicant talent	Is confirmation with VP written or verbal?
Staffing vendor manages interviewing and hiring tasks	Background or driving investigations not updated prior to hiring
Unit managers prepare written detailed job descriptions	Quarterly orientation sessions might lack relevance for some staffers
Confirms request to hire with unit VP	
Adopts standardized job titles/pay rates	

Strengths

Jackson's choice to contract with a staffing vendor is a smart move. News of job opportunities can be placed in a national database and draw transportation professionals from across the country. The applicant pool would be more qualified and independent, and the staffing vendor should have more flexibility to select finalists for interviews. With its shift of lower value-added work related to advertising, answering inquiries, and interviewing to the staffing vendor, Katy Hoogerland gains time to focus on higher value-added activities: interacting with new hires.

Detailed job descriptions are presented to Hoogerland by the various unit managers (for instance, accounting manager, parts manager, marketing manager, special handling transportation manager, etc.). These requests, made in writing, explain the needs of the position and help ensure the proper candidates are vetted by the staffing vendor. Having them in written form improves the recruiting subprocess because Jackson Transportation and the staffing vendor rely on the same details about work expected of the applicants.

Hoogerland seeks approval to search for a temporary hire from the vice president of the unit (e.g., operations, administration and finance, marketing). This discourages a unit manager from making unnecessary requests for new hires.

Jackson Transportation structures its work roles according to standardized job titles and fixed pay rates. This deters managers and unit vice presidents from bringing in new staffers under *ad hoc* job titles and with higher salaries or hourly wage rates than approved for those positions. For unionized workers, these would need to be in line with local, regional, or national norms.

Weaknesses

Although authorization to move forward with the temporary hire is confirmed with the unit vice president, we do not know if the approval is made in writing or orally. If a verbal confirmation, this is a weakness because it does not provide concrete documentation of the decision (approval or denial of the position request). Confusion could result if a spoken comment from a unit VP was misunderstood by Katy Hoogerland.

The staffing vendor undertakes all required employment, criminal, and regulatory checks on workers it sources to Jackson Transportation. But when the six-month probation period concludes and Jackson decides to extend a permanent hire opportunity to a worker, Hoogerland does not update the background checks. Jackson relies on investigations performed half a year earlier while the staffer was not legally employed by Jackson. Now that the employment situation is changing, Hoogerland ought to verify – at a minimum – that the staffer has a clean driving record and current licensing certifications. An employment check might not need to be conducted, but a review of criminal activity also can be warranted.

Company orientation for new hires is useful, but when offered quarterly some of the sessions might lack relevance for staffers brought on board two or three months before. A discussion of benefits and company policies should occur upon hiring. Additional human resources topics (e.g., sexual and discriminatory harassment awareness, diversity training) could be presented periodically during the year.

Fiona Colgate and Katy Hoogerland know several changes need to be made to internal controls over recruiting and hiring. Colgate brings experience from a large national carrier and can share examples of best practices with Hoogerland. But what about payroll?

Chapter Core Question 2: How does data move through the payroll subprocess?

Payroll Subprocess Data Flows

If there's one subprocess about which your typical staffer is passionate (and coincidentally serves as a built-in internal control) it's got to be payroll. After graduating from high school I worked at a large regional newspaper. Hired at the outset to be a general-purpose accounting department staffer, I rotated through all of the areas of the office (A/R, A/P, payroll, circulation accounting, newsprint accounting, and the cashier's office). Yet not many months after my arrival an unexpected resignation occurred and I was chosen to fill the position of head payroll clerk.

Imagine being responsible for the correct processing of weekly paychecks for a staff of approximately 1,500. Pay rate changes, requests for vacation pay in lieu of vacation, jury duty pay, changes in tax withholding, updates to benefit plans, staffers on short-term disability, new hires, and terminations all had to be accurately updated so the net result would be correctly translated into the dollars and cents that would be distributed to everyone on Wednesday afternoons.

How do your staffers act as a strong payroll subprocess internal control? As long as they worked a typical week they knew – to the penny – the amount of their net pay. If a mistake was made or a processing error occurred staffers would sometimes be the first to know and report it to me. If someone's net pay was $289.44 each week but she received a check for $308.71, she would come up to the fourth floor and ask to talk with me. I could examine the payroll register and see that the staffer had received a $25.00 award, for example. She'd reflect, "oh yes, I won the April Suggestion of the Month Award and forgot it would be included in my paycheck this week". Of course, when staffers' net pay was less than they expected, you could be sure to be questioned by the staffers, too!

Payroll data's journey starts with staffers logging their hours worked, moves to supervisors who review those hours, and ends with the clerk's role in processing paychecks. Databases maintain tax tables, benefits data, wage rates, and records of staffers' current and period-to-date payroll data. There are as many ways of organizing the payroll subprocess as there are business entities so a comprehensive look at data flows in payroll is impossible. So we will concern ourselves with Jackson Transportation's bi-weekly payroll subprocess. In particular, the focus is on the timekeeping, payroll processing, and net pay distribution tasks. We could incorporate this with connections to the human resources department (salary enhancements, updates to tax withholding documents, changes in benefits and other voluntary contributions) but that's straying from our more concentrated examination of the payroll subprocess. Nonetheless, all of these tasks that originate in the human resources office impact the calculation of staffers' net pay. Making sure these updates are entered into the payroll subsystem in a timely and accurate manner is the responsibility of someone in either the human resources department or the accounting department, depending on where "payroll" is housed.

Fiona Colgate meets Jackson Transportation's payroll manager, Nicole Villars, in Nicole's office on a Tuesday afternoon. "It's the quietest time of the two-week pay period", says Villars, as she places a bag of popcorn into the microwave in the nearby kitchenette. Nicole notes that there are two methods for collecting timekeeping data. "Truck drivers and driver's helpers – they're constantly on the road in a truck – use one approach. Everyone else uses another method," says Nicole. Fiona asks first about the way truck drivers and their helpers submit their time data.

Villars explains that each truck driver uses a smartphone to access a website, built by the Jackson Transportation IT staff, that allows drivers and helpers to enter their bi-weekly work hours and for the drivers, the number of miles driven in the period. At the end of each two-week pay period (a Saturday), the scheduling managers for the consumer/business division and the special handling division review the hours and mileage logged by the drivers and helpers. These are matched against the register of scheduled trips and analyzed for reasonableness. The two managers investigate unusual discrepancies between the budget (schedule) of hours/mileage for the two-week period and the actual data submitted. If the managers feel follow up is needed, they phone the drivers and discuss the factors that caused the difference from the schedule. "Perhaps there was an accident which caused the driver to make a material detour on a planned route, or bad weather forced the driver to sit idle for hours," Nicole says. After the managers are satisfied with the information, or if they make adjustments when they feel the drivers are taking advantage of a situation, managers approve the hours and mileage at the timekeeping website.

> Staffers enter hours worked at a timekeeping website linked to Jackson's accounting information system

For those staffers that don't work on the road (they're called *resident* staffers), bi-weekly hours are entered at the timekeeping website. Supervisors access the website to review hours entered by their subordinates. Questions about work hours are discussed face-to-face with staffers, and after inquiries are answered in a satisfactory fashion those hours are approved by supervisors with a click of a mouse. Other than the way the timekeeping data is entered at the website by the two groups of staffers (desktop computer v. mobile phone) the tasks are the same.

On the Monday following the pay period end, Villars generates a trial payroll register from the payroll module of the accounting information system used by Jackson Transportation. She scans the gross and net pay amounts for reasonableness and investigates odd situations. These are confirmed, or if an error is found, corrected in the payroll module. When her review is complete she prints a final version of the payroll register. Then she prints paychecks for staffers working at the corporate office. Paychecks are signed using a check signing machine. Nicole has possession of the signature plate used in the machine and retrieves it from a locked cabinet separate from the machine. In addition to the plate, she grabs a clipboard on which a log of machine counter numbers is kept. She notes the starting number on the non-resettable counter on the machine, installs the signature plate, runs the paychecks through the machine, jots down the ending number on the counter, removes the signature plate, and locks it and the clipboard in the cabinet.

After lunch, secretaries, supervisors, and managers from Jackson's various departments converge on the payroll office to pick up paychecks for staffers in their departments. Those individuals are responsible for distributing paychecks to their department members at 3:00pm.

When all of these tasks are finished, Villars schedules an **electronic funds transfer (EFT)** of the net pay for the non-resident staffers: drivers and driver helpers. They receive their net wages via direct deposit on the Wednesday after the bi-weekly pay period end.

The payroll module maintains detailed data for the current pay period, quarter-to-date, and year-to-date periods. The company's former chief financial officer and the current accounting manager are pleased with the capabilities of the software and the way the database can be searched to retrieve relevant data for decision making purposes.

Fiona Colgate, listening as Nicole Villars describes the subprocess involving timekeeping and preparation of paper paychecks for the resident staffers, draws the data flow diagram in Exhibit 10.1. She knows she will refer to it in her effort to identify areas for improvements in efficiency and internal control.

Chapter Core Question 3: What are possible internal control trouble points in the payroll subprocess?

Payroll Subprocess Internal Control Trouble Spots

STOP. Refer to Exhibit 10.1. Think about the situations contributing to internal control weaknesses in Jackson Transportation's payroll subprocess. Find a partner and jot down your ideas using the tabular format from prior assignments. Be sure to include suggestions about ways to detect or deter the internal control weaknesses. Please don't read on until your partner and you have finished your work.

Exhibit 10.1 – Jackson Transportation's Resident Payroll Subprocess DFD

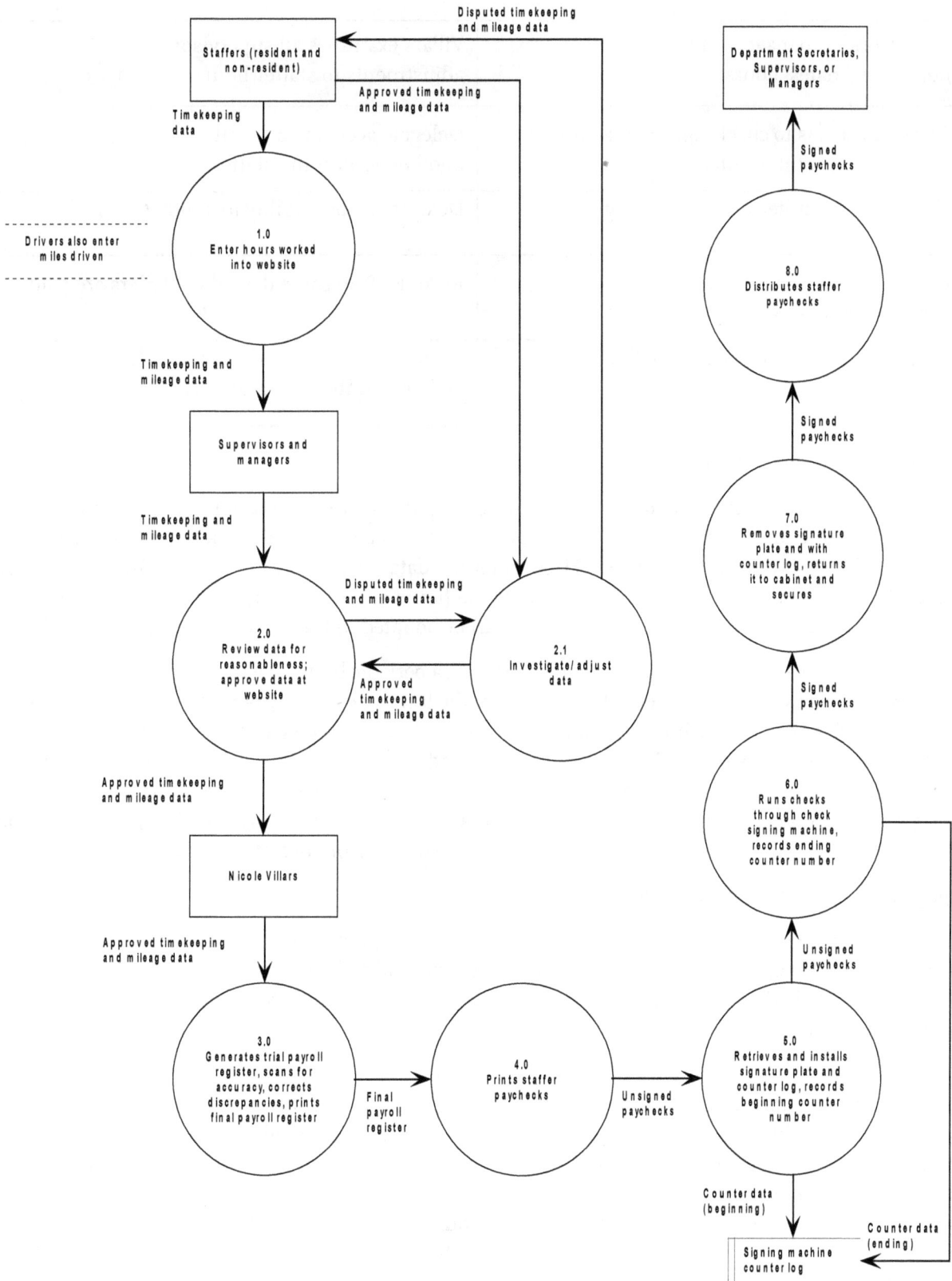

Internal Control Weaknesses	Suggested Internal Controls
Staffers can falsify hours worked	Villars uses trend analysis on staffers' hours to highlight unusual patterns
Supervisors or managers can alter subordinates' hours	Villars examines all supervisor adjustments to staffer hours
Villars has access to check signing machine signature plate and counter log	Delegate access to a secretary or another accounting staffer
Villars writes counter numbers on log	Delegate responsibility to another staffer
Drivers and helpers paid two days after resident staffers	Make EFT on same day other staffers are paid
Paper checks used for resident staffers	Switch to EFT/direct deposit for all staffers, on-the-road and resident

Staffers can falsify hours worked

No matter which device they use to enter their hours, all staffers run the risk of inflating the number of hours they enter into the timekeeping application. Supervisors and managers cannot be expected to accurately track their subordinates' time (otherwise, let THEM enter the data instead of the staffers). One internal control is already in place: supervisors and managers review the hours entered and investigate unusual circumstances with their subordinates. Another internal control can be adopted in the payroll office, however.

Nicole Villars can perform some analytical procedures on a periodic basis. She might randomly select 10 percent of the staff to review each pay period. She would scan the last five or six pay periods' data to see if any irregularities surface. These should be investigated by talking with the supervisors and then the staffers. Will it prevent over-reporting of hours worked? No. Remember that nothing will stop fraud. Rather, it is the role of internal control to deter or discourage or detect (raise awareness of) weaknesses, problems, and inefficiencies. So if a staffer was intentionally inflating his work hours but word spread that the payroll office periodically audits the timekeeping data, this might discourage the majority of staffers from overstating their hours.

Supervisors or managers can alter subordinates' hours

Who's to prevent a supervisor or manager from acting inappropriately and using the timekeeping review and approval step as an opportunity to change (add or reduce) a subordinate's recorded hours? Suppose a supervisor wishes to retaliate against a subordinate and reduce his hours. Maybe the supervisor hopes to obtain some favor or positive feedback from a subordinate by increasing her hours. How would the payroll office know the manager is acting inappropriately?

The frequency of supervisor adjustments to the timekeeping data ought to be few, thus Nicole could examine every change submitted in each pay period. Such review (verification) would alert all supervisors and managers that every change will be investigated, potentially discouraging authorizers from abusing their roles. If she's studying each change every pay period, Villars will pick up on patterns involving certain managers and can approach them about their actions. Once again, this could act as a deterrent to alterations. Repeated problems should be referred to the human resources director, Nathan Glendale, who could approach Fiona Colgate and the unit vice president for the offending manager.

Villars has access to check signing machine signature plate and counter log and writes counter numbers on the log

These two internal control weaknesses can be assessed together. Villars' access to the check signing machine and the signature plate, along with her responsibility to record the number of signature imprints made (*i.e.,* checks signed) gives her complete control over preparing payroll checks, signing payroll checks, and logging the number of checks signed. Without a segregation of duties for the check signing task, Nicole could easily print additional payroll checks for herself and others and cover the fraud since asset access and recordkeeping are consolidated with one person.

How can this be remedied? Perhaps the secretary for Nathan Glendale, Fiona Colgate, or Lee Jackson can be tapped to maintain possession of the signature plate. Payroll checks cannot be signed until Villars and the secretary, together, access and install the signature plate in the check signing machine. As well, the secretary would note the starting and ending number of the machine counter and reconcile them to the number of payroll checks that were signed. The check signing task is strengthened by adding a segregation of duties and verification control.

Drivers and helpers paid two days after resident staffers

Not so much an internal control weakness as it is an unfair or unnecessary business practice, non-resident staffers ought to be paid on the same date as those who work at the corporate facility. Electronic funds transfers (direct deposit of net pay) are nothing novel or complicated and do not require additional days' preparation to handle. In fact, it is more efficient and a stronger internal control for the accounting manager to arrange one – instead of two – transfers of cash from Jackson Transportation's checking account to its payroll **imprest account**.

Paper checks used for resident staffers

Jackson Transportation already uses electronic funds transfer (EFT) for non-resident staffer payroll. Why doesn't it extend this internal control technique to the benefit of all staffers? Electronic funds transfers improve internal control; fewer hands come in contact with paper paychecks. Reflect on the Monday afternoon scene in Villars' office. Secretaries, supervisors, and managers stop in throughout the early afternoon to pick up paychecks which they, in turn, hand to their staffers. In between the time they are picked up from the payroll office and distributed to staffers, paychecks might be dropped, lost, misplaced, or stolen. Once the checks leave the confines of the payroll office, how are they safeguarded by those who have them in their possession? Are they locked in a drawer until 3:00pm when handed out? Or are the paychecks laying on a desk, free for the taking?

Jackson's control over its most liquid asset – cash – is enhanced by paying all staffers through electronic funds transfer.

Caveat: Direct Deposit Internal Control Risks

While it seems electronic funds transfers for paychecks can eliminate several weaknesses in internal control, new problems might be created. If the person authorizing the payroll funds transfer (at Jackson Transportation this is Nicole Villars) also has the ability to set up new staffers fictitious or ghost staffers could be created and their "wages" directed to the fraudster's bank account. Similarly, when staffers are terminated but not removed from the direct deposit system, their wages could continue to be "paid" through manipulation of the trial payroll register and also sent to the fraudster's bank account.

To compensate for a possible lack of separation of duties, a staffer independent of the human resources department and not involved with payroll tasks (someone from the accounting function but without general ledger or cash disbursement responsibilities) should periodically review and match HR data, timekeeping records, payroll registers, and government unemployment reports. This would highlight discrepancies between employment and payroll records. A summary of

> Electronic funds transfer has its own set of internal control challenges

the work could be prepared for the chief financial officer and human resources director. If the entity is large enough, its internal audit staff would be in the ideal role to carry out such inspections, in which case the results would be reported to a member of the board of directors or trustees.

Chapter 10 Concluding Thoughts

Recruiting and hiring qualified staff is a continual challenge regardless of the size, type, and nature of an entity. Government units like public school systems, not-for-profit organizations such as the Osborne Senior Center, global for-profit retailers like Natureza.com, and Wolf River Hardwoods, a small, family run specialty manufacturer face difficulties when they advertise for and interview new staff. As fictitious trucking company Jackson Transportation did, using a staffing contractor and adopting a temp-to-hire model can provide various internal control benefits and financial and operational advantages.

Once staffers are brought on board and the entity takes full responsibility for paying them, internal controls over the payroll subprocess are critical. Every organization desires to correctly and promptly pay its staff. But in the haste to accomplish this, internal control problems can pop up. Relying on a combination of current information technologies and old-fashioned care and independent oversight, entities can attain both desires. Through a combination of appropriately placed authorizations and supervision, segregation of duties and evidence, and asset access restrictions and verifications, human resource business processes can be efficiently carried out and with reduced risks for fraudulent behavior.

We've come to the end of *Fundamentals of Accounting Information Systems: An Internal Control Approach*. My purpose for writing this simple textbook was to acquaint students with a collection of topics on data flows in various business processes and the internal controls commonly associated with those processes. I hope I succeeded on both counts. Errors and omissions in the material are solely my responsibility.

Chapter Core Vocabulary

Electronic funds transfer – the movement of cash from the bank of one entity to another entity's bank using telecommunication networks. The Federal Deposit Insurance Corporation defines[29] it as "any transfer of funds, other than a transaction originated by check, draft, or similar paper instrument, which is initiated through an electronic terminal, telephonic instrument, or computer or magnetic tape so as to order, instruct, or authorize a financial institution to debit or credit an account".

Human resources business process – activities conducted by the human resources department encompassing recruitment/hiring, career development, training, payroll, benefits administration, and government reporting.

Imprest account – a bank account set up to hold an exact amount of cash for a temporary and specific purpose. For example, if the net bi-weekly payroll for Jackson Transportation is $189,365.91, the accounting manager would approve a transfer of this exact amount from its general-purpose checking account to the payroll imprest account. When all payroll checks have cleared and payroll direct deposits authorized, the balance in the imprest account will be zero. This internal control helps ensure that only legitimate payroll disbursements can be paid from the account.

Read It, Do It – Sabará Construction

Objectives

---

29   FDIC Law, Regulations, Related Acts. 6500 Consumer Protection, Section 903.7. Federal Deposit Insurance Corporation website. Available at : http://www.fdic.gov/regulations/laws/rules/6500-1350.html

To recognize internal control weaknesses in the payroll subprocess and make recommendations to strengthen them.

To understand how restricting access to assets and incorporating independent verification strengthens a system of internal controls.

Introduction

Sabará Construction was founded in 1974 by three brothers, José, Roberto, and Victor. Sabará specializes in commercial construction such as small shopping centers and franchised restaurant buildings. Operating in Oklahoma, it was a successful business. However, when José married a woman from Minneapolis, Minnesota, and Victor met and married a college classmate from Cheyenne, Wyoming, the brothers wanted to honor their wives' wishes to move closer to their families. The brothers decided to investigate these markets to see if Sabará Construction would be able to compete in them. It did, and shortly after the firm developed a reputation for reliability and quality construction. Sabará Construction presently serves clients in its original state of operation plus Colorado, Minnesota, Montana, North Dakota, and Wyoming. Sabará Construction is headquartered in Tulsa, Oklahoma, and has regional offices in Cheyenne and Minneapolis.

Payroll

The nature of construction work makes it necessary to hire many workers for short periods of time. Sometimes when one job is completed the workers are shifted to another project site. Other times, completely new groups of workers are hired.

Employees are paid bi-weekly. Whenever a new job site is established, the site manager receives a box of blank timecards that have been mailed from one of the regional Sabará offices. If the site manager runs out of timecards before the end of the project, the manager has workers document their hours on sheets of notebook paper. Workers fill out their timecards daily, and leave them inside the trailer that serves as the site office.

On the last day of the pay period (Friday), the site manager reviews the timecards, discusses any discrepancies with workers, signs the timecards (or sheets of paper), prepares a payroll summary sheet, and faxes the payroll summary to the regional office. On Monday, each regional office's payroll clerk prepares payroll checks, which are then reviewed and signed by Victor (Cheyenne), José (Minneapolis), or Roberto (Tulsa). Afterward, the clerks organize the paychecks according to job site and mail them via U.S. Postal Service overnight mail to the various post office boxes for the Sabará Construction job sites. The site managers retrieve the paychecks from the U.S. Post Office locations on Wednesday, and leave them in the job trailer for workers to pick up.

Required

You are an associate with the international public accounting firm Kidd, Bloomfield & Napier. Sabará Construction has engaged the firm to perform a comprehensive study of its accounting processes. Your role on the team is to review the payroll activities and suggest ways to strengthen its internal controls and operating efficiency. Please present your analysis and suggestions in a memo to Caleb Hartong, your manager at KBN. Your suggestions will be incorporated into the larger report prepared for Sabará Construction.